Spiritual Warrior

Uncovering
Spiritual Truths
in
Psychic
Phenomena

SWAMI KRISHNAPADA

HARI-NAMA PRESS

For information address:

Hari-Nama Press
P.O. Box 4133
Largo, Maryland 20775

ISBN: 1-885414-01-3
L.C.C.: 95-081991

Cover design by Greg Golem

Spiritual Warrior

Uncovering Spiritual Truths in Psychic Phenomena

Other works by
Swami Krishnapada:

The Beggar
Meditations and Prayers on the Supreme Lord

Leadership for an Age
of Higher Consciousness
Administration from a Metaphysical Perspective

This book is an offering to my spiritual mentor
His Divine Grace A.C. Bhaktivedanta Swami Prabhupada
in celebration of the centennial year of his appearance.

Contents

Foreword

O ne of the great questions facing modern society is how to reconcile different religious traditions. The conflicts between competing religious doctrines and metaphysical systems give strength to the skeptical argument that religion is simply a product of human imagination, with no basis in truth. Even if a person wants to follow a spiritual path, what is he to believe?

This book, *Spiritual Warrior*, by Swami Krishnapada, presents a universal approach to religion and spiritual growth that attempts to reconcile several important spiritual traditions. The book's underlying philosophy is taken from the Vaisnava tradition of India. However, the book is aimed primarily at people influenced by a number of other traditions. These include Christianity and Islam, the mystery schools of ancient Egypt, the spiritualistic traditions of Africa, and the many supernatural and quasi-supernatural manifestations of the "new age."

Two basic approaches to the problem of religious diversity are the *exclusive* approach and the *inclusive* approach. According to the exclusive approach, ideas which differ from a given set of accepted religious doctrines are rejected as invalid. This approach simplifies things for those who can fully place their faith in a particular set of doctrines. It can be of great value for some people, because it allows them to imbibe the wisdom of their particular tradition without distraction. However, for people who are doubtful and confused by many conflicting claims, religious exclusivism may act as a barrier to spiritual progress.

The inclusive approach attempts to unite diverse schools of thought by combining them together. According to this idea, different traditions are describing the same reality from different perspectives. Even though some accounts may be corrupted or adulterated with false material, one can arrive at a consistent picture of reality by combining different traditions and noting their strong points and their common features. This is the method used in this book.

What picture emerges if we try to combine different traditions? Swami Krishnapada emphasizes a basic three-tiered picture of reality based on the world of gross matter, the world of subtle material energy, and the transcendental world of pure spirit. Paralleling this is a three-tiered picture of ourselves (and other living beings) as combinations of gross physical body, subtle mind, and transcendental soul.

All truly spiritual teachings are concerned with the transcendental world. But the subtle realm is important because it has a great impact on our physical lives. The experiences of the conscious self after death depend on the subtle energies, and many religious traditions advocate the goal of attaining life in subtle heavenly regions. Finally, observations of subtle phenomena can increase faith in religious scriptures by providing empirical confirmation of old religious teachings. Thus, the subtle realm can be seen as a bridge connecting the world of gross material experience with transcendence.

Unfortunately, many manifestations of the subtle world seem fantastic from the modern point of view. Modern society is dominated by the so-called "enlightenment paradigm" of eighteenth century France, in which the rational mechanics of Isaac Newton was taken as the model for all of reality (a step Newton himself was not willing to take). Subtle energy also follows laws, but the flexibility with which these laws are manipulated by subtle intelligent beings often makes subtle effects seem absurd or impossible. This makes it difficult for us to have a clear understanding of subtle phenomena, and it gives an advantage to materialists who take their stand on the laws of physics.

Unidentified flying objects (UFOs) are an example of an apparently absurd or fantastic manifestation. Swami Krishnapada integrates UFO aliens into his comprehensive system, along with angels, Vedic demigods, and other traditional subtle beings. There is much to be said in favor of this approach, but it also creates some problems.

With thousands of people claiming they have been abducted by extraterrestrials (ETs), there can be no doubt that the UFO phenomenon is real and important. Even total skeptics should regard it as a sociological development worthy of serious study. But unfortunately, the subject of UFOs is troubled by an overflowing abundance of absurd and contradictory information. Some of this is due to manmade hoaxing and disinformation, but some of it also appears to be due to the UFO phenomenon itself.

Swami Krishnapada emphasizes that subtle beings are not necessarily well-motivated. He points out, for example, that the beings involved in psychic healing may, in some cases, be harmful in nature. The same considerations apply to UFO aliens and to channeled communications from various "higher beings." These phenomena may involve real agencies that are part of the subtle dimension of reality. But some of these agencies may be deceptive or, at the very least, not interested in giving us the truth. For this reason, it is advisable to place information deriving from UFO encounters and psychic phenomena under the heading of "empirical data" and not directly incorporate them into a definitive metaphysical system.

As empirical data, this information can give useful insights showing the relevance of old scriptures that many people regard as mythological. For example, Swami Krishnapada describes UFO mother-ships that are involved in the guidance of affairs on this planet.

It is interesting to note that mother-ships are clearly described in ancient sanskrit texts. For example, the Shiva Purana describes three flying cities created by an engineering genius from another planet, named Maya Danava. It goes on to remark that "Aerial chariots shining like the solar sphere, set with Padmaraga stones, moving in all directions and looking like moonshine, illuminated the cities." Modern accounts also describe a large craft surrounded by smaller glowing vehicles.

Swami Krishnapada points out that religious truth should be evaluated on the basis of authorized scripture, living saints, and bona fide spiritual masters, or *gurus*. When pursuing the inclusive approach to the problem of religious diversity, there is always the danger of adulterating the knowledge that this three-fold process is intended to conserve. But one can avoid this problem by carefully distinguishing between different categories of evidence.

The basic claim of religion is that knowledge of spiritual truths beyond our sensory grasp is descending to us from the spiritual world through the aid of various higher beings. At the same time, there are beings more powerful than ourselves who are deceptive and inimical. This means that we ultimately have to develop the power to discriminate between different sources of information. .Swami Krishnapada emphasizes the need of personal purification to attain this power of discrimination. For pessimists, I should remark here that even though it may seem very difficult to do this, a world view that allows for the possibility of obtaining real spiritual knowledge is much more encouraging than the world view of gross materialism, which reduces all knowledge to meaningless patterns of interacting atoms.

The idea of organized deception brings us to another theme of Swami Krishnapada's book: the role of various manipulators in controlling and exploiting human populations. According to some conspiracy theories, secret organizations of humans are controlling ostensibly democratic governments, and these secret societies may have connections with unfriendly extraterrestrials. This is clearly an idea fraught with paranoia and disinformation.

It is also a very old idea. For example, the concept of ETs controlling human governments can be found in the ancient sanskrit literature of India. The basic plot of the historical epic called the Mahabharata is that the earth was once taken over by ETs who took birth in earthly royal families and consolidated their power in the human kingdoms of their day. In response, the demigods, led by Krishna, also took birth on the earth and engaged in a struggle to drive out the inimical forces.

The idea of a struggle between forces of good and evil is found in many religious traditions, and in the Vaisnava or Vedic tradition of India it appears as the battle between the *devas* (demigods) and the *asuras* (demons). Swami Krishnapada maintains that such a battle is going on now on this planet. He connects this with millenarianism—the idea that as the twentieth century draws to a close, there will be a period of turmoil and disaster culminating in a new age of enhanced spirituality on this planet.

There are many rather doubtful prophecies about coming earth changes, and the date of 2000 A.D. is tied explicitly to Christian chronology. But this date is given some confirmation by a sanskrit text called the Brahma Vaivarta Purana. There, the goddess Ganges asks Krishna what her destiny will be in the age of *Kali*, after Krishna departs. He tells her that for 5,000 years, people will be relieved of their sins by bathing in her waters. He then points out that sins are immediately reduced to ashes by association with pure devotees of Krishna who chant His holy names. Krishna says that His devotees will be on earth for 10,000 years of *Kali*. According to traditional Indian chronology, 5,000 years of the age of *Kali* have now passed. So it is time for the 10,000 year period of Krishna's devotees to begin.

After describing many categories of intelligent beings in the universe, all with unique natures and desires, the ancient text called the Srimad Bhagavatam pointed out that "due to the great variety of desires and natures among human beings, there are many different theistic philosophies of life, which are handed down through tradition, custom and disciplic succession. There are other teachers who directly support atheistic viewpoints."

The great variety of religions is evidence of our inner diversity as conscious beings. But just as we all share a common spiritual essence, the ultimate spiritual purpose of all great religions is the same. To bring out this ultimate purpose in the context of diverse contemporary concerns is the goal of Swami Krishnapada's book. This is certainly an important goal in these troubled times.

Dr. Richard L. Thompson,
Bhaktivedanta Institute
Author of: *Alien Identities: Ancient Insights into Modern UFO Phenomena*

Editor's Preface

S *piritual Warrior: Uncovering Spiritual Truths in Psychic* *Phenomena* is composed of transcribed lectures on metaphysical phenomena presented by Swami Krishnapada. Because the topics were originally presented as lectures, the format was quite different from a written style. In the editing process, we modified the text towards a written style to enhance readability, yet at the same time preserved some of the verbal nuances to maintain the mood of the original presentation. We hoped to create an atmosphere where you are literally transported to the audience, experiencing the powerful presence of the speaker, Swami Krishnapada, while being fed essential food for the soul.

Other stylistic considerations should be noted. First, although we recognize that God as the absolute person encompasses both male and female, the masculine form is used when referring to God to emphasize the position of God as our Father. Second, when speaking, Swami Krishnapada rarely says "I" when referring to himself. He uses the plural "we" based on his knowledge that what he offers is not of himself; he is simply a messenger who is sharing information given to him. In this sense, when he speaks, it is many people speaking rather than just one. Other times he may use "we" in a way that includes himself with the audience/reader.

Third, as Swami Krishnapada examines various psychic phenomena, he brings in perspectives from varied spiritual philosophies. He often uses sanskrit terminology from the Vedas, a vast body of ancient scriptures from the area that is present-day India. Finally, at the end of each chapter we have presented some of the many questions and answers that were exchanged during the original lectures. We hope that this will answer some of the questions that you might have and will give you different angles from which to view the presented topics.

The selections in this book are part of a much larger collection of lectures that will be published in subsequent volumes. We hope you make the most of these and of the upcoming lectures in the *Spiritual Warrior* series. This information is very rare. If taken seriously, it can greatly improve the quality of your life.

Author's Preface

We are living in an era when everything that can go wrong is going wrong, yet at the same time miracles and extraordinary events are becoming commonplace. These occurrences reflect the increasing polarization of consciousness on the planet: opportunities for total absorption exist on either end of the pious-impious continuum. This era is very special. Despite strong negative influences, an upgrading of global consciousness is taking place. Barriers between planetary dimensions are being removed to allow assistance in ushering in a "New Age"—an age of spiritual rejuvenation and enlightenment.

As we approach the twenty-first century, millions of people around the world have begun to have mystical or psychic experiences. Many more who have not consciously experienced such happenings are aware of the phenomena and are open to learning more. Even those who previously claimed disbelief in the topic find themselves reflecting more on the possibilities as they face ongoing exposure through the media. Metaphysical subject matter has established its identity on television, on the radio and in many diverse publications ranging from prestigious scientific journals to comic books. Paranormal experiences will increase as philosophers and religionists more closely examine universal truths, as people ask more soul-searching questions and as modern technology taps more subtle levels of awareness.

The purpose of this book is two-fold. The first is to present information that will encourage the reader to view the world from a perspective that is little explored, a perspective transcendental to conventional material or metaphysical analyses. The second purpose is to provide answers to long-unanswered questions and to stimulate new questions to assist us in raising our standards and goals. As we increase our standards, we will hold ourselves and others more accountable. Three important themes throughout the book are 1) the distinction between positive and negative psychic phenomena, 2) the distinctions among the physical, astral, and spiritual realms, and 3) our ability to create our own realities based on our consciousness. We must all be spiritual warriors armed with practical knowledge and skills to spiritually fortify us during these challenging times. In this way, we will be preparing for the transformation to come and can serve as agents of positive change. Those who are willing to make this commitment to spiritual growth will benefit the most from this book.

Acknowledgments

I wish to express deep gratitude and thanks to all the people that committed much time and effort in the production of this book. There were many services involved and many who gave their assistance in the transcribing, typing and proofing of this book: Yasoda Mensah-Dzomley, Martin Mensah-Dzomley, James Parks, Courtney Parks, Laurice Stewart, Olivia Cook, Millard Hawkins, Sylvester Brooks, Arlene Brooks, Ayodele Brooks, Aisha Abdul-Wakil, Patricia Jackson, Ida Michael, Krishnanandini Dasi, Eric Akridge, Paul Ewing, JoAnn Noble, Lisa Ratcliffe, Graham Land, and Michael Smith.

Special thanks to Steven Rosen, Marilyn Wood, and Paulette Bowles for editing assistance, Adam Kenney for the layout and Greg Golem for the superb cover design.

1

Dreams:
A State of Reality

O n the average, people spend at least one-third of their lives asleep. While asleep, all of us dream, although we may not remember our dreams. It is important to understand exactly what is occurring while we are in that altered state so that we can use that time of sleep to enhance our functioning in the waking state.

The Body, the Astral Body and the Soul

Ancient scriptures tell us that man is more than the physical body. In fact, we have two bodies: the physical and the astral, or subtle. But we are the soul! According to the ancient Vedic scriptures of India, the size of the soul is 1/10,000 the tip of a strand of hair. It is located in the heart region and is the actual life force. The physical, as well as the astral or subtle body, acts as a covering or costume that the soul wears in its journey throughout the material sphere. As we pass from costume to costume or from body to body through the process known as reincarnation, the impressions of previous lives imprint themselves on the subtle body and are carried with us during each lifetime. In the dream state, activity in the subtle body becomes more dominant than activity in the physical body. Our dream experiences are often impressions accumulated from many lifetimes.

Four Types of Dreams

Dreams can be classified in many different ways. We will examine four types. The first concerns dreams that occur as a result of physiological stimulation. Although your body is asleep, your senses are still active, allowing sensory stimulation to enter into and influence your mind. For example, you hear a train whistle which is internalized in the subconscious and becomes a fire engine in your dream.

The second category involves thoughts that are dormant in the subconscious. Whatever you think about often becomes impressed upon your subconscious mind. You are not conscious of these thoughts in the waking state, they are lying dormant; but during sleep, when the conscious mind is at rest, these thoughts express themselves. The mind is still active when the physical body is asleep so the thoughts have an outlet for free expression. What you experience while asleep is often a release that did not, or could not, take place in the waking state. Dreams can give you a clue regarding what you are preoccupied with internally and the degree to which you are being affected by your various environments.

The third type of dream concerns the predominating thoughts you have when you are awake. If, for example, you are impoverished and constantly hungry, most of your dreams will be about food and finding food. In Western society, the two most dominating concerns are work and sex, so most dreams will be focused around these. A person who concentrates a great deal on the opposite sex will experience more sensual dreams than one who does not have this focus. The images portrayed in the media also heavily impact our thoughts, awake and asleep. Sometimes one's dreams are about family, depending on how close the family relationship is. Often, when people in a close relationship are separated, they can contact each other in the dream state. Many times situations you experience or people you know are on your mind when you go to sleep, which directs the course of your dreams.

The fourth category of dreams involves those that help to work out *karma*, that is, lessons that are to be experienced in this lifetime. Sometimes, dreams can be used as a medium to play out the *karma* that one has accumulated. Situations that would normally have had to be lived through in the waking state can be quickly worked through in the dreaming state, thus saving time. The dream medium can also provide the opportunity for advanced beings to chastise you. This serves two functions: one, it saves time because the dynamics do not have to be played out in the physical realm and two, the lessons learned through the subtle body penetrate the soul more thoroughly, leaving lasting impressions.

Outside the Body

When one's subtle body travels outside of the physical body during the dream state, this experience is sometimes referred to as lucid dreaming. When metaphysicians are able to do this at will, the phenomenon is called astral projection or astral traveling: the ability to consciously leave the physical body and project the subtle body beyond its physical limitations. There are systems derived from ancient schools, such as the Vedic and the Egyptian traditions, that teach this as an exacting science. Students are taught to move beyond the limits of the physical body to tune into more subtle levels. This perspective places emphasis on the fact that one is more than the body and that there are numerous levels of reality that allow many higher connections to be made.

There is beauty as well as danger when you deal with the subtle realms. The beauty is that you can have realizations, revelations, and experiences that can carry over into the waking state. The danger is that you can expose yourself to negative influences. There are many positive as well as negative entities that infiltrate one's consciousness while dreaming or disturb one during astral travel. Often they appear in the form of family members or close friends. There are also beings on the subtle plane that are in the habit of engaging the sleeping person in unwanted sexual activity.

Ghosts, or disembodied beings, are one type of negative disturbance. A ghost is a living being that has left its previous body prematurely due to events such as suicide or murder and has been denied access to a

physical body. Because the desire to enjoy is a fundamental characteristic of the soul, the subtle body
seeks any opportunity to inhabit a physical body to
satiate its gross desire for sense gratification. When
people allow their aura to vibrate on the lower fre-
quencies through activities such as drug or alcohol
use, they become likely candidates for contact with
these disembodied entities.

As you open up spiritually, your subtle body has a
particular effulgence which attracts entities from
both the divine and negative natures. You become
more sensitive and aware of everything. You become
more intuitive and have more experiences in the
dream state. If there are messages you should receive,
the impressions will always be there, even when you
are asleep, and you will act on them without consciously being aware of it. If a communication is really
meant for your growth, even though you may forget it
or may not be able to understand its significance, it
will still have an effect on your consciousness.
Ultimately, both the positive and negative experiences
are "quality tests" to assess your level of sincerity.

Influencing the Unseen

There are things that you can do to protect yourself from negative influences during sleep. It is helpful
to hang a picture of a saintly person in your home
since everything has energy in it. Place a picture of a
spiritually advanced person behind your bed as if it is
overseeing your physical body. The more spiritually
advanced the person, the more potency there is in
that person's photograph, and the more of that

potency can be summoned to your aid. Negative entities will not feel comfortable disturbing you with a
saint's picture hovering over your head.

When you enter an environment that is different
from your normal sleeping environment, remember
that every single dwelling has the energy of the people
that frequent it. Some people, especially those who are
spiritually oriented, find it difficult to rest soundly in
hotels and motels. They are disturbed by the impure
energy permeating those environments, even if the
place has not been used for many months. It is healthy
to purify these types of environments by playing tapes
of spiritual music. By chanting, meditating, or even
putting up spiritual pictures for the duration of your
stay, you can transform the area into a place that
actually augments your spiritual consciousness. If
nothing is done to spiritualize the atmosphere, it will
be like walking into a room filled with poisonous
fumes. The converse of this is also true: by sleeping in
a spiritually surcharged atmosphere, dreams that offer
spiritual realization and assistance can be obtained.

If someone is frequently under attack by negative
entities, it is because of a polluted consciousness that
needs to be upgraded. A negative entity dislikes visiting a clean mind as much as a rat dislikes going to a
clean place. You can purify your consciousness by following the aforementioned suggestions and by maintaining stricter spiritual practices. Putting up spiritual paraphernalia around the home and not allowing
any negative activity to go on in the environment can
help you greatly. This may mean asking friends and
loved ones to refrain from drinking, smoking, taking

drugs, gossiping, or doing any activity that does not encourage spiritual thought and action.

If you are sensitive and find that you are constantly under attack, have nightmares, or feel your body regularly trespassed upon, it may not necessarily be due to entities that are cruel or vicious, but to ones that are seeking love and support, or are just childish and mischievous. In these cases, you can kindly and compassionately address the entity in your mind and invite it to meditate with you in your sacred space. Engage it in some spiritual activity, giving it a little push in the right direction. If your love and devotion are sufficient, you can literally liberate that soul from its state of bondage or incoherence. These entities need sufficient love and light to upgrade themselves and become spiritually successful. If the entities are vicious, fear gives them strength. As a spiritual warrior and light bearer, a loving person can fight such an entity in order to release its soul and send it on its way.

Maximizing Your Rest Period

It is important to remember that when the body tells you to sleep or rest, it does so because it needs time to rejuvenate itself. Therefore, getting proper rest will help all aspects of existence. Our eating habits have a significant impact on our lives, too. If you eat heavily before going to bed, your body has to work harder to digest the food. It does not get the rest it needs, and thus, you are more likely to experience negative dreams. Try to eat no later than three hours before lying down. If you want to maximize the nourishing benefits of sleep, you should try to go to bed before 10 p.m. The most powerful hours to nourish the body through sleep are between ten and twelve at night. Some of you who sleep a lot and still feel tired should try altering the hours of sleep. If you want to sleep fewer hours and still get quality sleep, then sleeping between ten and twelve at night is best.

Consider your state of mind—your consciousness—before going to sleep. This is extremely important. Make a commitment to spend at least fifteen minutes spiritualizing your consciousness before going to bed. Read something spiritual, listen to spiritual discourse or music, or engage in discussion on a spiritual topic. Push aside the chaos and confusion that were a part of your day, and focus on spiritual reality. In this way, you will prepare yourself for the next six to eight hours of sleep. If you allow yourself to focus spiritually, you will provide less of an opportunity for negative elements to enter your dreams. You can then most benefit from your sleeping state.

Sleep can also assist with problem resolution. You would be amazed to know that many major discoveries in human history have resulted from revelations that occur upon arising. People first reflect on a particular problem before resting. During sleep, they concentrate on the problem on an unconscious level. When they awaken, they have the resolution to the conflict or problem. Part of what happens when the physical body is at rest is that you become more receptive to higher beings that serve as your guides. No one is a solitary agent. We all have various types of guides who assist us. Most important, there is a form of God in everyone's heart, and when you put the physical body to rest, you make closer contact with the Lord in the heart and with your higher self.

Maximizing Your Dreams

Most people do not remember what happens during the dream state. One useful technique to help you retain your dream experiences is to lie still when you wake up. Once you move your body, you integrate back into the physical dimension and you lose contact with the subtle realm. When you awaken, before getting out of bed, immediately reflect upon your experiences of the night before. If you wait even five minutes, you will forget. Some people keep a journal by the bed to record and later interpret their dreams.

Keep in mind that the practice of dream interpretation is not generally useful for spiritual advancement. There is a current trend where people are encouraged to write down every single dream and analyze every symbol. This practice can be misleading because each component in a dream can have varied meanings. Look at the example of a snake. A snake is interpreted in different ways by different cultures. In parts of the world where snakes are seen all the time, they do not stimulate fear as they do in this country. In other parts of the world, snakes are part of rituals and are considered sacred. There is not one universal meaning of a snake in a dream. People codify things and events as positive or negative based on culture. Even within a culture there can be variations of codification. Thus, dream analysis by the average person often can lead to confusion due to personal speculation and mental gymnastics.

There are many spiritually advanced people who, due to long-standing practices such as meditation, have caused their subtle body to become more sensitive. Thus, they may have certain insight into dreams. However, this is not the case for most people. Dreams that are of distinct spiritual significance should be given attention. Do not be concerned with interpreting mundane dreams that you may experience. Examine dream patterns and what they mean to you personally. You are the director of your dreams in most cases, and so when you have certain kinds of dreams you can discover their meanings.

One beneficial way to use your dreams is to direct them to areas of your personal and spiritual growth. As you enter into the dream state in a spiritual consciousness, you are more likely to have a dream that is productive and that will accelerate your growth. This usually requires the guidance of someone who is spiritually advanced. As you raise your consciousness, this process will get progressively easier. However, it is quite difficult if you are a spiritual neophyte. Also, if you raise your vibration to become more conscious of what you think in the daytime, you can have more positive dreams.

As your consciousness becomes more developed, you must become sensitively attuned to your inner and outer environment so you can receive higher knowledge and guidance. Some of you will be given spiritual guidance through the medium of dreams. A very significant dream of this caliber occurs between the disciple or student and the mentor or spiritual master. Often, there is a need for the spiritual master to warn the disciple or to give certain types of lessons that may not be easy to receive under normal circumstances. In such a situation, the communication will occur through the medium of the dream. Because you have been made aware of the opportunity for spiritual growth provided by dreams, you now will automatically receive more assistance from your spiritual guides when you are dreaming.

As mentioned, dreams can give you clues as to what you are most concerned about and how you are being affected by what is going on around you. In general, you should just try to become more spiritual in your waking state and you will have more spiritual dreams. As you grow spiritually, you will find yourself teaching more as you learn more. Your learning and your teaching will take place even in your sleep.

Question: How can we raise the vibrations in our homes to affect dreams in a positive way?

Answer: Because your house is your sanctuary, try to make your house a place of worship and behave in your home as an example to others. Don't let anyone come into your house who engages in activities like drinking or using drugs. Don't even let others feel comfortable smoking just because you love them or because they are close to you. You want to share the best you have with anyone who comes into your home. You wouldn't want to invite people into your home and give them poison such as alcohol or drugs or watch them take such toxic substances and just sit back and smile. You want those who come to your house to be elevated by the energy prevalent there.

The concern and love they feel in your house will inspire them to make changes in their own lives.

Don't feel intimidated about taking these measures, because if you really care about someone, you must remain unconcerned about how the person may perceive you. Friends or family members may feel disturbed that you won't take drugs, drink alcohol, or even eat meat with them, and that you won't let them do these things in your home. However, remember that caring about other people means that you don't want to see them do harm to themselves. If a person doesn't want to associate with you anymore, then you don't need that kind of association.

One of the most potent ways to spiritualize the home is to create a sacred space, an altar, or a room used only for meditation, prayer, or spiritual reading. If space is limited, a bookshelf or a corner will do. This is the place to keep your spiritual books and pictures and should be the place where you burn your candles and incense. Your sacred place will become an area of high spiritual vibrations which will affect the entire house, thereby attracting pious personalities. Having a sacred space will also remind you that your home belongs to God and that you are simply the caretaker of it.

Question: You talked about how outside experiences can influence our dreams. I had several unusual dreams after reading a book about a person who used to go into trance states. A lot of strange phenomena also began to occur like glass exploding or I would hear voices softly calling my name. So many strange things happened that now I refuse to read a book unless it has a strong spiritual message.

Answer: Just as there are higher beings who spread spiritual messages throughout the atmosphere by means of books, films, music, and other mass media, there are beings of a demonic nature who try to slow down the progress on this planet through these media. Exposure to books and media of this type can have a negative effect on you. Some of you may have experienced nightmares or other problems after reading or viewing such material. If you are a little psychic, their activities will have an even greater impact, because the more psychic you are, the greater the possibility of intrusion from the surroundings. Some of these entities are from other planets and some originate from the center of this planet. They are causing many problems in our culture. To counteract this, some of the beings of a higher nature write books or oversee the writing of books that enhance one's spiritual development. These books are considered fiction in a secular market but actually help to expand awareness of higher realms. These writers know that they will stimulate some readers and help unfold some *karma*.

Sensitive people must become more discerning about where they go, what they read, and with whom they associate. They are more likely to be drained by negative environments and are more likely to feel stimulated by positive influences. When negativity is present, more discrimination is necessary. Do not just read anything or go anywhere. If you pick up a book and experience an unusual sensation, put it down, especially if you are dealing with occult subjects. You may be negatively affected. Thoughts are saturated with energies that can intrude immediately or hover around you until they have an opportunity to take advantage of you. Thought forms that surround you at a particular moment may wait until a later time to affect you.

Question: How do we attract help from higher personalities through our dreams?

Answer: Since dreams are influenced by the predominant activities and mental preoccupations of the waking state, in order to attract higher beings you must engage in consciously higher activities. If we spend our days speaking verbal garbage and engaging in activities that do harm to ourselves and other living entities, why would any being of a higher vibration want to associate with us in our dreams or otherwise? Thus, if we raise the vibrations of our surroundings by meditating and acting according to a higher standard, utilizing prayer and focusing on helping others, we will be guided by those whose role it is to assist souls in their spiritual development.

2

Searching for Paradise

*B*ecause much of the traditional sacred information about the Supreme Lord and our interconnection with Him is no longer easily accessible on this planet, there is a great deal of misunderstanding about spiritual topics. One such area of confusion concerns what heaven is and what the kingdom of God is. We will examine this distinction beginning with a discussion of the material universe. By better understanding the material universe, we can better appreciate and understand the heavenly planets and the spiritual world.

Where in the Universe Are We?

According to the Vedas, the universe in which the earth is situated consists of a fourteen-planet system. The specific planets are categorized into three areas: higher planets, middle planets and lower planets. The lower or hellish planets are abodes of extreme chastisement for the purpose of rectification. The medium planets are the earth-like planets. The higher

planets are those heavenly kingdoms that people
sometimes call Heaven. Above all these planetary systems is the kingdom of God, or the spiritual world,
which is anti-material in nature and has nothing to
do with the mundane world. Science, specifically exo-
biology, says that there are billions of other universes,
many of which contain life molecules. Our planet is
actually like a speck of dust floating in one of the
smallest universes in the creation. By considering our
minute position in the larger scheme, we can be more
open to aspects of this discussion that may seem completely outside of everyday reality.

Agents of the Lord

In every universe, there are agents in charge of
overseeing the basic functioning of the material energy. They all work under the Supreme Lord. The Lord is
not actively involved in the creation and maintenance
of these universes. Agents of the Lord called demigods
are responsible for these environments. They oversee
the material universes under the Lord's jurisdiction
[see chapter three].

One such agent is called Brahma. Different names
are given to the same being according to different
traditions. In the Vedic tradition, Brahma is the name
of the agent that is assigned the duty of creation, a
chore we usually ascribe to the Supreme Lord. More-
over, he is responsible for overseeing some of the
heavenly kingdoms and resides in the highest of heavenly kingdoms. There is a different Brahma for each
universe. When people speak of God the Creator, they
are actually referring to Brahma (by whatever name

each respective culture chooses to call him). He is not God but is serving a function on behalf of God.

Brahma's post is given to an agent who sometimes falls from higher abodes or falls from the spiritual kingdom but does not fall very low. At other times, the post is given to a being who is almost 100 percent perfect but has not completely transcended the tendency to be in control. Such a soul is given a chance to channel those desires by being a co-creator with God and being responsible for seeing that the material manifestation of the universes take place in the proper manner. Everyone has had the opportunity to occupy the same post as Brahma, but because of association with material energy, cannot remember. Some of you may have had that post for millions of lifetimes.

Brahma has a life span of 311,000,040,000,000 (311 trillion 40 million) years. Such a number may seem fantastic, but consider how your view of time and space is relative to your body. A small ant would see the distance from one wall to the other as being tremendous, but to an elephant it would be just a few steps. What to speak of those beings who are the size of a planet, or of those beings who *are* the sun, the moon, and the earth? Yes, the earth that we call Mother is itself a living entity. Just as you are a universe with living entities, like bacteria, inside of you, so too is this planet. When you start letting your mind consider these things freely, you will see that there are so many aspects of space, time, and different dimensions, and that it is all relative.

Since Brahma is a material being, albeit a very advanced one, he too leaves his body at the end of his life span. When he leaves his body after 311 trillion years, all creation is annihilated in his particular universe. Every four billion years, all the planetary systems are completely destroyed, including the top heavenly planets. Within those four billion year periods, there are fourteen distinct intervals of temporary annihilation. This is the rhythm within which organized and systematic creation, maintenance, and annihilation take place. Every two thousand years, there are also some major shake-ups. Those on the earth planet are in the introductory phases of a major shake-up that is about to come to a head very soon. Many of you have come to this particular planet and universe at this time to play a role in this transformation. Exposure to this type of knowledge will help you to unfold and understand your future purpose.

The Eternal Cycle of Four Ages

Each universe experiences a cycle of four different ages, called *yugas* in sanskrit, that are much like the seasonal changes present on earth. Just as the seasons are characterized by the amount of light and heat available, the *yugas* are distinguished by the amount of God-consciousness that the residents are exhibiting at the time. Their consciousness ultimately influences the general life span, mental state, and standard of living available to the population. We are presently in the fourth age, called the age of quarrel and dissension in some teachings, an age of massive chaos and pandemonium. This age is called *Kali* in the

Vedic scriptures. This is a time marked by more intrusion from the subtle plane in the form of fairies, disembodied spirits, ghosts, and other entities. In this age, many people are possessed and people exhibit their most animalistic tendencies.

During *Kali yuga* one can expect to live at most up to one hundred years or so, but as the age progresses, a person will be considered old at age thirty. Consider a teenage girl who has led a rough life of prostitution and drug and alcohol abuse. She could easily look twice her age. Thus, our lifestyle, our thoughts, and how we take care of the physical and subtle bodies has an effect on how the aging process manifests in our bodies. People will become so gross, and life will become so hellish that despite scientific advancements, life spans will continue to decrease.

We are only five thousand years into *Kali yuga*. It is scheduled to last for approximately 430,000 years before the general process comes to a conclusion and we move into the next cycle. There is much to expect with the end of this cycle. The Vedas describe much famine, drought, and starvation, so much so that people will become cannibals. Don't be shocked; there are hundreds of thousands of people who practice cannibalism right now. There are people in governments around the world who make human sacrifices and sometimes eat certain human organs as a way of obtaining power. In fact, many cosmetics presently on the market contain human tissue from fetuses, with the claim that these will slow down the aging process and rejuvenate the skin. Whether you use human organs for dinner, cosmetics, or something else, it is still human tissue, and to use it in these ways is demonic.

In this age of quarrel, little children carry guns to school as a way of solving arguments or protecting themselves. This is an age when the retort "I'm going to blow your head off" must be taken seriously. When people reach into their pocket to pull something out, it is no longer just brass knuckles or a chain; in many cases it is a gun or a knife. These signs show that this age is moving rapidly, even though we are only a few thousand years into it.

The age before *Kali* was called *Dvapara yuga*, and its duration was about 800,000 years. This age was more God-oriented. People lived to about one thousand years of age. The Bible speaks of Methuselah's longevity; at that time, people were graced with a longer life span. The physical size of people was also larger when the spirituality was deeper. Descriptions exist of the Sons of God, who were angelic entities that many would consider to be giants. Over time as the spirituality decreased, so did everything else. The memory, the intelligence, the compassion, the love, and the longevity all began to decrease.

The age before *Dvapara* was the *Treta yuga* which lasted about 1,300,000 years. In this age, people lived to be about 100,000 years old, and they practiced elaborate spiritual rituals. The age prior to that was called *Satya*, or the golden age. This age lasted for almost 2,000,000 years, and the citizens of this age were the most God-conscious of all.

Everything is an aggregate of individual and collective consciousness. In different periods of history, a certain kind of personality predominates; the souls in those periods have similar experiences. For example, the souls that were very active during the 1960s have similar mentalities. Adults who were born during the baby boom have similar perspectives and life goals. There is a certain mentality among the present-day children. This situation occurs because specific souls come at particular times according to the work they have to do; therefore there are some similar patterns.

Paradise Found?

Now that we have a better understanding of the functioning of the our universes, let's examine the heavenly planets. We said earlier that there is a difference between the kingdom of God and the heavenly planets. In the Koran when Prophet Muhammad made his ascension, he traveled with the Angel Gabriel first to the lower hellish planets and then to the heavenly kingdoms up to the Seventh Heaven, which is the highest material planet. At that point, Angel Gabriel could not go with him any further. Prophet Muhammad then went to Sidratil-Muntaha, which is beyond the heavens; it is in the spiritual world, the abode of Allah. There he had personal association with Allah. Angel Gabriel wasn't allowed to go to that level because he was not properly qualified. Prophet Muhammad was able to have that experience because of his level of purity and dedication to the will of Allah.

When we talk about heaven, we are talking about places or states where intensified and unceasing pleasure is available. These experiences are available from the earth level up to higher planetary systems. Although such a place is called paradise, we are not really talking about the place where the Supreme Lord resides. We must make this distinction. When the Bible states that God created the heavens and the earth, one may wonder where God was situated when the heavens were being created. It can be logically concluded that there is a difference between the heavens and where the Lord resides. The heavens are a part of the material creation. The Lord resides in the spiritual world.

How is one chosen to go to heaven? The key determinant is one's consciousness. There are three basic modes or principles that permeate the material atmosphere and influence our consciousness. Based on our desires, one of the three modes will have a predominant influence on our mentality and consequent actions. The first or lowest mode is the mode of ignorance, which leads one to be aggressive, obnoxious, unclean, animalistic, exploitative, lazy, and manipulative. Those in this mode enjoy inflicting pain on others. People who have mainly lived under that influence will go to a hellish environment when they leave their bodies at death. They must spend some time there for serious adjustment and rectification.

Then there is the mode of passion. Persons in this mode are very attached to material gain, success, fame, and power. Those individuals are attached to family life and the material environment. Those who leave the body while in the mode of passion will normally come back to an environment that is predominantly self-centered. Such a place is actually not hell, but surely it is not a heaven.

The mode of goodness influences one to be pious, religious, philanthropic, compassionate and ethical. People in this mode try to love their neighbors as themselves. They are usually vegetarians and are greatly concerned with the earth and its inhabitants. When they leave their bodies, they have many opportunities to go to the heavenly kingdoms for various types of pleasurable experiences, which are like extended vacations. However, even residing in the heavenly kingdoms with all of their pleasures is only temporary. It is the payment you get for the pious activity performed.

It is difficult to go directly from the heavenly kingdom to the spiritual world because the lack of duality and suffering in the heavenly environments prevents the inhabitants from fully depending on the Lord. There isn't much opportunity for devotional service to the Supreme. In our present environment among the earth-like planets, there is more duality and contrast. The transitory nature of life on earth often increases one's frustration and determination to get beyond the temporary. Such a situation makes it more likely that one will cry out to God. Thus, it is less difficult to go directly from the earth planet to the spiritual abode than to go from the heavenly planets to the spiritual abode.

What Are the Heavens Like?

Although our responsibility is to lead you to the spiritual world rather than the heavenly kingdoms, we will describe some things about the heavenly kingdoms. The Bible describes heaven as a place full of light where there is no sorrow, or pain; there is only joy. In the Koran, or more specifically, in the Hadees-E-Qudsi, the heavenly kingdoms are also discussed. According to the Hadees-E-Qudsi, when one goes to the heavenly kingdoms, one will never age past thirty-three years. People typically don't like to grow old, especially when the aging process brings on all kinds of bodily and mental dysfunctions. So in the higher pleasure abodes you will not have to experience old age. Here one is constantly pursuing sexual involvement because orgasm is basically one of the highest of pleasures in these realms. In the Koranic description of the heavenly planets, it is stated that a man will be able to enjoy seventy virgins and that each person will have 80,000 servants. There are amazingly gorgeous women and extremely handsome men. Your sexual experiences on earth would be like pain when compared with those pleasures. In terms of childbearing, when there is a desire for procreation in the heavenly kingdoms, a child can be brought forth in a matter of minutes. The child is not a small baby, but a healthy and vibrant youth. There is also a special kind of intoxication there that doesn't leave an unpleasant aftereffect.

In the higher of the heavenly planets, the living entities sometimes live for millions of years, and in the highest of these, the living entities live for trillions of years. (Keep in mind, however, that this is all relative. It's all a matter of the time frame in which we view things as to whether we consider a time period to be short or long.) Many of the mystic abilities for which we hanker in the material world are common attributes of the beings of the heavenly kingdoms. They have the ability to make their bodies very small or very large, or even very light. Some of the heavenly beings can enter into this environment and reorient their atoms and molecules in order to manifest in certain ways. Some of these entities have the ability to travel to other planets or other universes and the ability to acquire things from outside of their immediate environment instantaneously.

Entities of the higher kingdoms have all of these abilities. These are just normal for them—the science of energy conversion. Some people who are now in this universe have the ability to summon souls back into their bodies—commonly called bringing the dead back to life—just as Ezekiel, Elijah and Jesus did. All of the demigods have this ability. Some of you have a hunger for mystic perfection because of the association that you have had in the past with agents of those heavenly kingdoms. You have an insatiable desire once again to be able to function on that level. Because of being too preoccupied with these mystic perfections, you have been denied access to them so there can be a focus on the real homework you are to do here. If you to want to focus on these perfections while on earth, when you leave here you will go back to the heavenly planets where those kinds of abilities are common.

In these higher planetary systems, a different aspect of God is worshiped according to the evolution of the beings on that particular planet. In some environments, the aspect of God with which people are familiar is the god of the sun, the god of the moon, the god of water, or the god of air. We can see the influence on this planet because even here some people are worshiping one of these aspects of the Godhead. In some cases it's due to some previous experience on a planet where that particular aspect is dominant and worshiped with reverence and distinction.

If the heavenly environment sounds exciting to you, then maybe that's what you need to pursue in this life-time. If it doesn't sound quite so exciting, consider that there is something even beyond that environment. These descriptions of the heavenly realms can give some stimulation, if you want it. Remember, though, that you'll be settling for a mere vacation, because life in the heavenly planets has to come to an end. Some-times after a vacation is over, you get more work than you ever expected, and you may even question if it was wise to have taken that vacation in the first place.

Opportunities for Higher Contacts

The challenges you meet on earth and in the heav-enly planets are all part of the growth experience you undergo in your endeavor to return to your original home in the spiritual kingdom. According to what you need for your own acceleration, certain kinds of impressions, realizations, and associations will come to you. Why seek to acquire mystical abilities when their possession does not necessarily imply wisdom? Knowledge can and should lead to wisdom. Wisdom means you go beyond the mundane and material into deeper consciousness to open up the heart. Wisdom means you no longer look aimlessly for God, the angels, or the higher beings, because you begin to realize that they were always with and around you. You were just not allowing yourself to see, hear, or associate with them, to be guided by them, or to be sufficiently protected by them. Thus, self-realization does not involve going out and acquiring something. It is a matter of opening up, receiving, and using what is already part of you.

There are persons in the world who are in constant communion with angelic beings. These beings give them information that allows them to do things that are beyond the normal scheme of activities. As mentioned, you don't have to focus so much on how to see these beings or even on how to see God. You do, however, have to understand that such beings see and notice you, so you must purify yourself in order to eradicate the coverings that are denying you association with them. These associations occur in some rare cases, such as on space missions when astronauts have had sightings. Because these people were outside their normal earthly environment, these types of experiences were more accessible.

The living entity is wandering from lifetime to lifetime—sometimes in the earthly kingdoms, sometimes in the heavenly kingdoms, sometimes in the body of a man, sometimes in the body of a woman, sometimes in the body of an angel, sometimes as a demigod. Each individual is constantly exchanging one body after another for lifetimes—sometimes hundreds of thousand of lifetimes, sometimes millions of lifetimes. As the intelligence pushes one's consciousness beyond the desire to simply gratify the material senses, one acquires enough intensity to come into contact with agents of the Lord. The Lord constantly sends representatives according to time, place, and circumstance to help cut some of the ropes that are binding us. This helps to free us of the amnesia that has caused us to forget our true nature and to not experience the blessings available to us. By having contact with the Lord's emissaries, one begins to make a major jump in consciousness and will soon be able to connect once again with the spiritual kingdom. What you do with that contact is up to you. Having that contact means you will never be the same. You cannot hear this kind of knowledge and actually think that you are going to continue as before.

This information is like a time bomb. It's a seed that has been planted, an opportunity that has been earned. You cannot suffer from amnesia, regain your memory and find it easy or comforting to forget again. This information has been given to the soul. It is only a matter of time before the soul begins to act upon the stimulation it has received. If anything is said that you do not feel comfortable with, just file it away, as if for someone else. Don't become disturbed. If anything is said that challenges your tradition, don't put up a wall; just accept that right now you are situated where you are. If, however, something that is said adds to your tradition or acts as a catalyst to open a door for you, go through it!

We have purposely put out knowledge for those of you who have spent many lifetimes in the heavenly kingdoms or who are still caught up in trying to acquire the mystical perfections. This knowledge will enable many of you to interact with the angelic hosts when they come. When the angels associate with you, you will be receptive and able to use the empowerment made available to you. These beings we are speaking about come in their pure, complete states and you will have a chance, if you are ready, to join them.

Just as different countries all over this globe are operating on different times of day, every universe is operating on a different time schedule. In one universe, a particular cosmic manifestation is just beginning; in another universe, everything is coming to an end; and in yet another, the material manifestation is unfolding. The Supreme Lord resides in His own abode, with His loving associates. As you enter and join that association, all remaining sins and confusion are wiped away. As the love, guidance, and compassion of those associates spills over onto you, all that is negative within you is destroyed. All the last traces of greed, all the last patterns of frustration and fear, all the last questions of whether or not you are loved by God and what your purpose is . . . all of those concerns disappear. You begin to experience actual love in your associations. Loving relationships then become real and you begin to know what it means to be home again.

Question: What kind of techniques can we engage in that will reveal to us these loving experiences that you talk about?

Answer: A powerful technique is calling on the name of God. All of the major scriptures of the world emphasize the calling of God's name. The names of God have a profound effect on the material energy. They act like a weapon, cutting out much of the contamination that stagnates the consciousness. The names of God have the ability to convert material energy into spiritual energy. They have the ability to invoke the presence of the Lord. When you call out for someone, you are summoning some of the essence and presence of that particular person. The person's image comes to your mind, along with the particular attributes and traits of that person. The more spiritually advanced that individual is, the greater the reciprocation and the deeper the impression that contact with their name will leave. Similarly, when you call on the name of God, the sound vibration provides the all-powerful cleansing and purifying effect of God. There is a whole science and culture based on the calling of God's name, but in essence these factors are why it is important as a special key in the transformation of consciousness.

Question: Based on the understanding that the universe goes through cycles and that the living entities incarnate back and forth, a lot of the religious systems on earth anticipate that there will be a time when our material plane will begin to take on certain characteristics of the heavenly realms. Some people who are into astrology acknowledge this time as the "Age of Aquarius," and the biblical concept is one of the "coming of the kingdom of heaven on earth." What is the difference between incarnating in the material realm during this kind of cosmic cycle versus incarnating in a heavenly realm?

Answer: There is very little difference. As we explained, because the universes are all going through the cosmic cycle at different times, one could very well incarnate on an earthly planet, while it is in the stage of *Satya yuga*, or the golden age. Alternatively, one could incarnate on a planet in the heavenly realms. In either case, both environments would be similar: heavenly. That is why we emphasize that attaining the heavenly planets should not be the goal. Rather, the goal should be attainment of the spiritual world, which is permanent. The earth is going through a massive purification. You will find that a heavenly environment is gradually going to develop right here. Through this cleansing process many entities that are not of a high enough caliber to remain in the earth environment will have to leave and be reborn on the hellish planets or elsewhere. Those entities that have upgraded themselves, who are seeking heaven on earth, will remain here. However, there will be a major change in consciousness, with an emphasis on understanding our relationship with the Godhead.

Think about this: the whole process of birth, death, creation, maintenance and annihilation of the universes all takes place in one single inhaling and exhaling of the divine breath of the Supreme Lord. The dynamics of the universes are much, much bigger than we could ever imagine. Thus, it is critical that we remain open and receptive to all assistance and opportunities for growth. This will be preparation for the changes to come.

Question: Every world religion has some concept of heaven as the goal of their practices, as you have pointed out. What, then, prevents us from recreating chaos in heaven when we get there, just as it is on earth?

Answer: In order to obtain residency in a heavenly realm, one undergoes an upgrading transformation of consciousness. So certain lower-level thoughts and activities must cease and be replaced with higher conscious thoughts and activities. However, the heavenly planets are in the material plane, and spirit souls in material bodies are prone to the four material defects of making mistakes, being illusioned, having imperfect senses, and having a tendency to cheat. Our desire for sense gratification will bring us eventually to the kinds of distress that we are experiencing here. The key is to understand that even the heavenly planets are temporary, and that the only place we can find lasting uninterrupted happiness is in the spiritual world where material contamination is conspicuous by its absence.

3

Angels and Demigods

*E*ach person is a wholistic being who *has* a material aspect and a metaphysical aspect, but who *is* the soul. The problems of the world are so great that they cannot be addressed by looking at just one aspect of our existence. There must be an appropriate marriage between the material, the metaphysical, and the spiritual. This is not only healthy but it is imperative and necessary for survival. Angels and demigods are important in this regard, for they are forces who can assist us in surviving and advancing.

The Holy Books and Higher Beings

There are many dimensions to God's creation. There are lower hellish planets; medium planets; higher, heavenly kingdoms; and the spiritual world. There are many agents of the Supreme who are greater than us, have a more subtle nature, but are not quite God. The angels and demigods are in this category. An analogy is the President's cabinet. The President has many cabinet members who oversee

different departments. There is a difference between
a cabinet member and the actual head of state, the
President himself. Demigods, or *devas*, are the Lord's
cabinet members. They oversee the affairs of the
material world. People often mistakenly identify the
demigods, or those who are empowered to represent
the Divinity, as the actual Divinity Himself. Angels are
of a pious nature, as are the demigods. They differ
from demigods in that angels are not serving in
administrative positions.

Various scriptures refer to angels and demigods.
Let's begin with the Bible. Genesis 1:1 says: "In the
beginning, God created the heaven and the earth."
Genesis 2:1 says: "Thus the heavens and the earth
were finished and all the host of them." If God created
the heaven and the earth, we can understand that He
existed somewhere else, and brought into existence
the heavens and the earth from His own abode. The
heavenly planets are actually where the angels and
the demigods reside. The Supreme Lord is above the
heavens, in the spiritual world [see chapter two]. Both
the demigods and the angels are material beings but
are more subtle material beings than earthlings.

From this, we may go to another point. In Genesis
1:26, we find something quite astounding, which we
have all heard countless times: "And God said, let us
make man in our image, after our likeness, and let
them have dominion over the fish of the sea, and over
the birds of the air," and so on. The "us" in this verse is
plural and shows that God is not existing alone. If
God does not exist alone, who is He talking to? He is
talking to the demigods. They, as the Lord's cabinet
members, are taking responsibility for the creation of

the beings in the material universes. It is the demigods who say: "Let us make man in our image. Let us create a being in our image who has the ability to make spiritual progress. Let us advance the position of the earthlings so that they have more of a chance to aspire toward the Godhead."

As earthlings we are not a part of the original creation. The living entities on this particular planet are part of a secondary creation. It is just like a drama where after Act 1, the curtain closes. Then there is Act 2 and the curtain closes again. Similarly, there is always creation, maintenance, and annihilation in the material universes, and then the curtains close. Then the entire process is repeated again and again. Only the spiritual kingdom is always existing, unperturbed by the vicissitudes of time.

Let's examine one more point in the Bible. Genesis 6:1-2 says: "And it came to pass, when men began to multiply on the face of the earth, and daughters were born unto them, that the sons of God saw the daughters of men that they were fair, and they took them wives of all which they chose." This indicates that there were contacts between the sons of God, or the demigods, and the daughters of men. This interaction produced humanity as we know it.

The Koran also discusses angels. The Prophet Muhammad was able to give the knowledge of the Koran because of his contact with Angel Gabriel. The Koran discusses angels coming to this world and presents their realizations and revelations, which vary according to time, place, and circumstance. For example the Koran, Chapter 2, Verse 177 says: "It is not righteousness that ye turn your faces towards East or West; but it is righteousness to believe in Allah and the last day and the angels..." While belief in angels may not be as universal as a belief in the Divine Being, it is accepted generally in all major religions.

Angels in Action

There is a difference between angels and other entities such as ghosts. A ghost can be a disembodied entity, a being that didn't quite make the transition to its next physical body. Even though it doesn't have a physical body, the desires for carnal involvement still persist. For this reason, it tries to enter and use a physical body. A ghost performs pranks and basically has the same mentality as it did in its last embodiment. The ghost of a highly mischievous and devious person will emanate the same kind of disturbance as the individual did while in the physical body. A ghost will make you fearful. If a ghost is present in your room, you will feel as though a breeze has just entered. If you are touched by the ghost, you will experience a sensation of coldness.

When you come into contact with an angel, it is not because the angel is lost as is a ghost; the angel is on a specific mission. The angel may give you a blessing, a benediction, a warning, guidance, and even protection. An angel is not trying to enter into you and work through your physical form for sense gratification or to engage in pranks at your expense. The presence of the angel gives you a sense of warmth, security, solace, and comfort. Angels have always been helpers to the material universe.

You may know from biblical studies that an angel appeared to Abraham to stop Abraham from slaying his son. An angel descended to close the mouth of the lion when Daniel was thrown into the pit. An angel appeared to take Peter out of incarceration. Angels appeared to the Prophet Muhammad. These examples reflect the role of angels as a helpers of humankind. The book of Revelations emphasizes the coming of different types of angels. There are many scriptural references to angelic interactions.

Sometimes one may have difficulties distinguishing between a helpful guide such as an angel and an entity that has its own selfish agenda in mind. A simple way to evaluate these beings is to discern whether they are pious or impious. The efforts of the pious ones are directed towards assistance. The impious ones are literally trying to bring stagnation into your life.

If you have contact with an extraordinary pious life force, don't waste time trying to determine the exact type of angel. There are angels who are like babies or children, others who are feminine or masculine in manifestation, and still others who are of no sex. These specifics are not significant. What is significant is the message and how to use that message. Also significant is whether the contact is destructive or upgrades your situation. If you are attracting situations of a destructive nature, you have work to do to eliminate such association. If you hear voices and are becoming fearful, you must determine how you can upgrade yourself.

An angel is vibrant and full of illuminating colors. Such beings give you a tremendous sense of peace in distressful situations. When someone is about to have a near-death experience or is in a trance or a coma, an angel may intervene to ensure that the person does not leave the body. The angels commune with the person, telling the individual to return to the body to complete certain tasks. The angels describe what these tasks are. Events like these have always occurred and will continue to happen. Angels are appearing in our current day and age, especially to protect children. Sometimes children see them and report them. Other people who are sensitive or psychic also see them. Some people are aware of angels as constant companions who accompany them for the majority of their lives. For others, an angel appears to guide them out of specific difficulties. Some of you have heard of Michael, Gabriel, Uriel, and many other angels who become known according to their activities. They protect and provide loving assistance to the living entities in this universe and other material universes as well. The angels may not necessarily reside in one particular universe, since they have the ability to move into other arenas.

Activities of the Demigods

Demigods oversee the angels and the earthlings. As mentioned, demigods have administrative responsibilities. In ancient cultures such as Africa, for example, most of the worship was dedicated to the demigods. In many Third World cultures today, much of the worship is also dedicated to the demigods. As mentioned earlier, God has agents whom He has empowered to carry out certain functions for Him. The demigods can sometimes cause interference or conflicts in the material world, and so people worship them as a way to

pacify them. Sometimes Western scholars misunder-
stand this and they think that African cosmology
reveres many gods. There is one Supreme God, but
these traditions recognize the importance of the
demigods and the duties and roles that they perform.

Before Buddha came into this universe, there was
more interaction between the demigods and the people
of this particular planet. Priests would conduct rituals
to invite the company of the demigods. Buddha ended
many of the ritualistic activities because people began
to distort and misuse them. Buddha brought in a new
era which emphasized a lifestyle of nonviolence, ethics,
and moral responsibility. He brought about a focus on
a peaceful state of existence. This meant that he cur-
tailed excessive contact with the demigods and shifted
the focus from transcendence to peace. Although
demigods continually appear in our midst, we have
become less and less aware of them.

The *devas* are a large part of our day-to-day experiences. Astrology is under the jurisdiction of the *devas*.
No one on earth can produce the sun or the moon,
cause them to appear on a daily basis, or create the
basic minerals we find in the earth. These activities are
under the control of the *devas*. There has never been a
time when we did not associate with some of our higher brothers, sisters or parents from other dimensions.
There has never been a time when we have been left
home alone without higher contacts. There is definitely
contact today, as demonstrated by some of the current
space expeditions. Many of the astronauts from these
expeditions are now engaged in studies of these beings
because of their experiences in space. Some astronauts
have reported being followed by alien beings, and have

had tremendous realizations. Occurrences such as these will increase in the years to come.

The Need for Higher Assistance

The material universes are environments provided for beings who have chosen for various reasons to be outside their natural home. These universes are environments where we are imprisoned because of our envy of God. Life is nothing more than the process of reformation. Living in the material universes is like being in school; we are consciously or unconsciously attending different classes and taking various tests in the hope that we will finally graduate to the spiritual world. We have different experiences according to what lessons we must learn for our unfoldment.

Every major prophet tells us, as Jesus said: "Love not this world nor the things of this world." Why did prophets such as Jesus, Muhammad and Buddha place so much emphasis on the higher kingdom and disparage this world and all it represents? Why did they constantly tell us about rectification and reformation? Because, as ambassadors of the spiritual world, they came to enlighten us about how to graduate from the inferior material sphere and become situated in the superior spiritual realm.

Because the Lord is so merciful, He repeatedly sends us ambassadors to help enliven our consciousness. These great *acharyas* (spiritual masters) teach not only by their words but by their example. Human beings and the demonic forces have tried to cover up and corrupt their teachings in such a way as to pit religion against religion. All the major teachers have told us that we should love our neighbors as ourselves and that we should love God with all of our heart. They have also all told us that this world is not our original home. It is no accident that such diverse yet harmonious teachers have made this consistent, universal presentation. Consider how similar their messages have been: not one major prophet, not one bona fide teacher has said that this world is our home. Instead, these teachers have constantly emphasized that the kingdom of God is the real home that we seek. They are not just trying to get us to be escapists and run away from life. Instead, they are trying to bring us back to reality and to help us escape from this material prison. Although they come from diverse traditions, their message is the same.

Just as there are demigods and angels working on behalf of humankind, demonic agents are also extremely active in the world right now. There is a war going on at this time between the pious and the impious entities. Many of the earth changes we will be experiencing in the coming years will be due to evil entities making their last attempt to cause massive chaos and pandemonium. As a result of this, we are going to experience many more wars, both on gross and subtle levels.

The idea of a new world order, or of a one-world government, is not a matter of speculation. It is on the way to becoming a reality. The issue has become: who will control that one-world government, that one-world order? That is what the conflict is about between the pious and impious beings. The struggle between these two forces is causing many of the conflicts and transitions that individuals are experiencing at this particular time. This struggle may flare up externally as war. It may flare up as tribal tension. It may flare up as religious tension. They are all the symptoms of what is happening on the subtle level.

One of the most devastating weapons in this regard is mind control. As we enter the twenty-first century, we'll see that such subversive tactics will increasingly be influencing world citizens. However, angelic beings are also here doing their work. You may even recognize that you are a visitor yourself who has a tremendous amount of responsibility to help bring about a higher level of collective consciousness in this particular universe.

Preparing for the Future

As you are more open to assistance from higher powers, you will begin to have certain experiences. You will start to have more activity in your dreams. Some of you will begin to feel some pulsation in the area of the third eye. This pulsation is due to the awakening of a *chakra* (energy centers in the subtle body) that has been lying dormant. The fields of psychology and anthropology emphasize that human beings use less than ten percent of their brain capacity. This means that many of our abilities remain unused. Day to day we witness paranormal events that traditional, empirical, reductionistic schemes of knowledge cannot fully explain. We see that some people are able to heal the sick. Some people are mental telepathists and are able to read minds. Some people have the sense of clairvoyance and are able to see into the future. Our present material scientific laws do not understand, and cannot deal with, these phenomena in their totality. However, we know that these paranormal occurrences do exist; we may even know people who have experienced some of them.

Because of the transition that the planet is experiencing and will experience for a long time to come, we can no longer hold back this kind of information. Many people need to be become more receptive as extraordinary phenomena begin to take place. In your lifetime, you are going to see an unusual kind of life force on this planet. You are going to have more contact with other-worldly beings than has happened for millennia. You are going to determine what the nature of life will be and what the future of the human race holds for all of us.

In these discussions we are not asking you to accept anything on blind faith. We are definitely asking that you not immediately reject anything either. We suggest that you do some research for yourself. Just ponder the basic points, investigate them and, most importantly, try to know better how to protect yourself against subtle forces so that you will not become a casualty. If you take these simple steps, you will be one of those who help to bring about a new era for humankind.

Question: Could you speak more about the role of different scriptures and guides in consciousness upliftment?

Answer: The Bible, the Koran, the Torah, the Vedas, the Puranas, and other scriptures, as well as the prophets, Muhammad, Jesus, Buddha, Zoroaster, Madhavacharya, and other great teachers all have a role to play in consciousness-raising. Of course, we sometimes encounter teachers that are not bona fide, but all the bona fide teachers have a similar type of responsibility. They give a certain kind of knowledge adapted to time, place, and circumstances that is ultimately geared towards helping humanity in its conscious evolution. If we look closely, we will see that the essence of these texts is very similar. The only differences lie with the way their practitioners codify the information.

All traditions have an exoteric and an esoteric aspect. The exoteric elements concern the externals of the philosophy. Exoteric practitioners are usually more sectarian and insecure, and they propagate the exclusivity of their religion. The esoteric practitioners seek a more profound religious experience. Going deeply into their bona fide system, they touch on certain universal truths. They do not view other religious groups as threats, and thus they have no difficulties with them. If we follow these great teachers who are perfectly knowledgeable about these higher truths, our elevation on the spiritual path is assured.

There are sinister forces that are not only pitching race against race and tribe against tribe, but religion against religion. The more empowered demonic entities have lodged themselves in religious circles, causing great conflict. Many of our present-day, so-called spiritual teachers are actually in connection with these demonic energies; some are actually possessed. Although a person may heal the sick, for example, this does not necessarily mean that the power to do so is coming from a divine source. One can invoke lower entities, which can penetrate one's consciousness and provide great psychic abilities. Such psychic power is ultimately used to incarcerate others and increase the number of material difficulties.

In the coming years we should all be more discerning about where the information we accept comes from. Examine the lives of the channelers, the mystics, the mediums, the astrologers, or the clairvoyants. What are they saying and doing? Are their messages uplifting and liberating? Are they focused on the culture of love and devotion, or are their messages concerned with power, control, and material manipulation? Look at their lifestyle. Is it exemplary or sinful in nature? By carefully scrutinizing individuals such as these, you can understand whether the path they are on is negative or positive.

Question: You mentioned demigod worship. Could you speak about ancestor worship?

Answer: What you worship is what you get. Suppose one of your ancestors was a murderer, a fornicator, or a thief. On one hand you have love for that person, but you don't particularly want to emulate that behavior or lifestyle. Worshiping ancestors blindly is a little dangerous. With the rise in Afrocentricity, and the reassertion of African culture, ancestor worship has increased. However, we should remember that the more we focus on worshiping and serving the Supreme, our own growth and spiritual acceleration will be shared with our ancestors, most of whom need our help in this way. Demigod worship and ancestor worship can be compared to bribery. When you are trying to avoid doing something, you pay a bribe. Sometimes the person you pay can deliver, and sometimes they are just bluffing you. It's a risk you take. Some people want to avoid surrendering their lives to the Supreme, so they limit their spiritual activities to demigod or ancestor worship. By explaining the demigods, the angels, the ancestors and their influence, we do not mean that you should worship them, but that as servants of the Supreme we should have great respect for them. Even though they are on a higher level than we are, they are still part of the material world.

Question: I have heard it said that sanskrit is a language used by the *devas*. Can you speak about how languages affect the mind?

Answer: There is a vast difference between the ancient languages and those we use today. Language affects thought. Those of you who speak more than one language are aware of the different moods evoked by each language. Some languages are more limited than others in the amount of themes and ideas that can be expressed. Words that can describe something in one language may not exist in another language to convey that meaning easily. Language affects how we perceive the world and also how we relate to the world. Modern languages are gradually losing their ability to connect with the spiritual, because they deal less with metaphysical and spiritual phenomena and more with the material realm. Thus you see that monks, priests, *yogis*, and medicine men will often use an ancient language to invoke certain impressions in the consciousness and to stimulate certain faculties.

Specific languages can also affect certain *chakras* and can penetrate the covers of material nature. In the material world the soul is covered by eight material elements. Five of these are gross: earth, water, fire, air and ether, and three are subtle: mind, intelligence, and false ego. False ego refers to the false identification of ourselves as material bodies rather than spiritual souls. Specific languages vibrate with the potency to penetrate these elements and reach the soul. Therefore, even if we do not understand with our intelligence or minds what is being said, and our false ego is resisting, the soul is getting the message that is meant for it.

4
Fire and Brimstone, Horns and Tails

The topic of the devil, demons, and the hellish planets is fraught with fears and misconceptions. For this reason, it is often avoided. However, we must understand these subjects in order to have a comprehensive picture of the material environment and function within it as productive spiritual warriors.

A topic such as this brings with it a certain amount of contradiction. We will claim that free will exists, and yet so does predestination. You will find out that there are many devils or demons, yet at the same time they do not actually exist! A place called hell will be discussed that is actually a state of consciousness. These statements may seem contradictory because of the limitations of our understanding. We are accustomed to viewing things in terms of "either/or." Something is either *A* or *B*. In the spiritual world, something can embrace two polarities simultaneously; it can be both A and B. So, please bear with the seeming inconsistencies, and you will gain a deeper understanding without unnecessary confusion and fear.

The Ideal Vacation Spot

Let's go on an adventure. Let's pretend I have a travel brochure in my hand and we are trying to decide where to spend a vacation. I'll describe a particular place and we'll see if you want to go there. Once we get to this environment, no one will be allowed to leave for hundreds and thousands of lifetimes. This environment is designed without human survival in mind and, once you're in it, you are constantly harassed by your mind, by other living beings, and by material nature. While there, you have to struggle to feed, clothe and shelter yourself. You are under many different types of oppressive governments where the majority of leaders are manipulative and exploitative. You are always experiencing some type of disease, you grow older every day, and you have to die. No matter how much you love yourself or how much you take care of yourself, you are still going to die. No matter how much you care for others, they are going to die too. In this environment there is always war and ongoing preparation for more wars. The basic philosophy is: I kill you, you kill me, we kill them, and they kill us. If I asked: "Would you like to come there with me? Lets have some fun," you would all probably respond with a resounding "No! I am not interested." Consider this: we are all presently living in such an environment right now, an environment that we

have all consciously chosen to come to—this material world!

Free Will Versus Predestination

One may ask: "If we are in this type of environment, do we really have free will? We don't want to
grow old or experience disease. We don't want to
struggle so much just to remain alive. So where is the
free will?" There is free will in that you are free to
make whatever choices you like, at least within the
boundaries described. Those choices, however, bring
consequences with them. Let's say you go to a restau-
rant to eat. You look at the menu and you request a
particular kind of soup. The waiter brings the soup to
you. When you taste it, you don't like it, and you start
complaining. The fact, however, is that you ordered it.
You may not have fully considered the combination of
ingredients or the competency of the cook, but that is
what you ordered and that is precisely what you got.
That is the nature of free will. We have the full ability
to make a selection; we can press any button we
please. However, when we press a button we have to
take responsibility for what happens. The reaction is
predestined, but is activated by our choice.

Thus, both free will and predestination are realities. We are responsible for every situation in which
we find ourselves. This conclusion is rather difficult to
accept, especially in today's modern culture which
trains us to find someone or something to blame
when things go wrong. Whether individuals are suffering from cancer, family conflict, lawsuits, or any
other major problem, they have actually brought it

upon themselves. Let's look at illness. Even modern medicine accepts that some illnesses are psychosomatic. The mind can and does affect the body; it affects all matter. The subtle affects the gross and the gross influences the subtle.

Our situations are arranged by higher agents to allow us to become tired of trying to manipulate the material energy. Due to not being properly appreciative of the beauty of relationship with the Lord, humankind is given a temporary arena in which to act out desires. This environment is designed to frustrate, disgust, and disappoint us, to make us contemplative and introspective. Ultimately it is meant to drive us away from the temporary world in favor of that which is eternal. This is arranged for us to finally realize that our happiness lies not in dabbling with the material energy but in serving the Lord unconditionally, thus becoming whole again.

Life is a game in which we are meant to reestablish our real identity. Unfortunately, we often play according to our own rules, like children who make things up as they go along. Children sometimes play in the streets. Although it is dangerous, it still has great appeal for them. By acting on this desire, they put themselves in a very precarious situation. Like children, we need to learn the importance of taking responsibility for our free will and the importance of using it wisely. Unless we do, we will never be able to reciprocate properly in loving relationships.

Free will is critical in a loving relationship because there cannot be love without the opportunity to oppose that love. There cannot be an appreciation without the opportunity to express it through choice.

If we are made in the image of the Divine, then just as God has free will, we must also have it. The difficulty arises in our inability to understand, or accept, that it is not beneficial to try to use our free will separate from God. This is because we are part and parcel of God, a tiny fragment of the whole, but we are not the complete whole. As part of the whole, our function is to serve the whole. The whole is certainly not meant to serve the part. For example, imagine if your stomach tried to eat on its own and told your mouth, "I'm tired of you always taking the food first. I think I should get it first." This would be impossible. A part cannot properly function separately from the whole. This is the natural order of the universe.

As we understand more and more how we are responsible for what we experience, we can then make arrangements to experience that which is more auspicious, and we will be able to access the things that we really need. It is important to focus more on what we need than on what we want, because much of what we want unnecessarily complicates our lives. The answer is to approach the Divinity in the mood of, "Thy will be done. Use me for Your purposes." Even higher than that sentiment is to request that God remove our free will so that we cannot even exercise it. We are then fully available for the Lord's service.

Why Do Bad Things Happen to Good People?

We will now examine the concept of evil. Someone may wonder: "But if God is all good and if nothing happens outside of God's control, then how can there be evil in the world? How can an all-merciful,

beneficent God bring in, allow, and be responsible for
evil? On the other hand, if something does happen
outside of the Lord's control, does this mean that evil
is as powerful as the Lord? Could the devil actually be
supreme?" The answer begins with the premise that
God is all-good and all-loving. It is true that millions
of people do not even have clean drinking water.
Millions of people are dying from starvation. Millions
of people are refugees. There are famines, droughts,
hurricanes, and wars everywhere. Diseases decimate
the world's population. How do we explain these
occurrences? Consider a prison. When you go to
prison, you understand that it is not a vacation spot
or a palace, nor is it supposed to be. A prison is an
environment for rehabilitation and rectification, not
enjoyment. This material world is a prison, its nature
being one of suffering and misery. There will always
be wars in the material world. There will always be
disease and death. These phenomena are not natural
because we are in an unnatural position. We do, however, have within us the ability to rectify the situation
through the proper use of our free will. To the degree
that we identify with the material, or the unnatural,
evil is a reality for us. Evil is as real and as penetrat-
ing as one's perceptions and thoughts. If our consciousness is pure, we realize that the only reality is
the spiritual world. The more materially contaminated our consciousness is, the more the material world
with its misery and pain has an influence on us.

So evil does not exist, and at the same time this
whole material cosmos is fueled by evil. The low global consciousness at this time has attracted this evil,
and God allows it to remain. Why? Because suffering

the consequences of one's behavior can push one towards the absolute good, just as chastisement from parents can instill the correct behavior in children. One may view parental chastisement as negative, but it is actually an expression of love. People draw chastisement to them based on actions they commit, but it should be viewed less as an imposed punishment and more as a natural result of improper action. This type of thinking helps us to appreciate the opportunities for growth that our challenges provide.

Due to a misunderstanding of these issues, people believe that God and evil are mutually exclusive concepts. Seen from a more transcendental perspective, however, these two opposites are integrally related, as the two sides of a coin are related. Again, we all have the choice to serve God or to focus on serving ourselves. The reason we are in this prison of misery is because of our desire to serve ourselves. For choosing not to serve God, we receive painful reactions.

Demons: Who the Devil Are They?

The devil is said to be the one who causes evil in the world. Children are sometimes coerced to behave by threats that the "boogey man" is going to get them. As an adult, the boogey man becomes the devil and the fear remains. Devils are as real as you want them to be. However, if you refuse to give them power, then there is nothing much they can do to you. The insane person thinks a stick is really a snake and acts accordingly. A sane person understands, sees the stick, and is not afraid. Similarly, we have created so many things that are real for us only because we have allowed them to be real. What takes precedence in our lives is based on where we focus our energy. There are so many situations we have accepted as priorities that are, in fact, of little importance. Conversely, there are many very important priorities that we have blotted out of our consciousness. This shows how powerful the mind is. The mind can act as our own personal demon if we let it. If we mentally accept something, we have to act upon it. For example, if someone tells me "Swami, you are so ugly that it hurts my eyes to see your face," I can respond in various ways. I can accept the words at face value and become angry and furious. I can feel I have to respond to the person in kind. I can look in a mirror just to see how ugly I am. I can go to see a plastic surgeon. I could do all kinds of things. Or I can simply not allow myself to identify with that attack. If I don't accept it, then I don't have to engage in any activities to counteract it. I don't have to prove anything; I don't have to modify my behavior in any particular direction. Once we identify with the mind by accepting what the mind serves out, then not only do we accept the thoughts, but also the corresponding feelings, associations, conditioning, and behavior patterns. Like it or not, we accept the whole package. We must find ways to prevent identifying with, and being taken in by, the mind so that we can always make everything that happens a part of the growth experience.

There are many types of negative influences. One type of influence is thought forms. Every thought that is created by the inhabitants of this planet makes its way into the ethers, the subtle aspect of the air.

Thought forms take on a life of their own, influencing individuals and collectives. The more negative the thoughts, the more negative the influence. The more positive the thoughts, the more positive the influence. Like attracts like. The individual's consciousness becomes the group consciousness, which manifests as the collective consciousness of the planet.

We can make our minds the home of unfriendly beings. These beings are the source of those little evil voices that linger in the back waiting for someone to tune their consciousness into them; they are those risk-takers that drive us to endanger our own lives and the lives of others in foolhardy antics. These voices belong to subtle entities. There are three ways to react to what one is hearing: reject it outright; accept it as real and blot it out; or accept it and act on it. The amount of resistance that one has to these negative thought forms will determine which action will be taken. Those with less resistance can be influenced by negative energy because they have allowed themselves to tune into it. The voices become the reality for them, often with insane acts as the result. If we choose to reject negative messages, not only will these entities have no influence on us, they will not be drawn to us in the first place. Therefore, we will not make them a reality.

A relationship with negative energies can also occur through involvement in occult activities such as seances. Even if this activity is undertaken as a joke, it is dangerous because seances can attract demonic energy. Those that take part in seances and similar activities sometimes perceive negative entities and can be possessed by them. The amount of people engaging in satanic worship is on the increase; the church of

Satan is growing rapidly. Some of the top military government officers are in the church of Satan as are some of the top entrepreneurs, while some secret societies pay allegiance to the devil.

These days we must fortify ourselves against the evil that is available in the atmosphere. At one point in history, the forces of good and evil did not occupy the same universe. Humanity's spiritual resolve was pure and determined enough to keep good and evil separate. Over a period of time, sin permeated the atmosphere and good and evil began to associate not only in the same universe but later within the same planet and eventually within the same individual. These higher and lower selves that individuals now embody are constantly battling for control. The mind constantly flirts between one polarity and the other, being controlled to some extent by one's surroundings and associations. Currently, for many people the lower self is becoming dominant, and these individuals are becoming increasingly sinful. The higher self is becoming covered with lust, anger, and greed. People are gradually losing the ability to control and manipulate their own bodies. They are losing their independence and are becoming puppets of their mind and senses. We must examine this enslavement because what we focus on while alive directly relates to what the focus will be at the time of death—and beyond.

The Soul: At Death and Beyond

Before we discuss the hellish planets, we want to briefly examine the death process. The concept of preparation for death was greatly emphasized in the ancient culture of Egypt, or Kemet, as it was originally known. This is because much of the life process is about preparation for the death experience. The Egyptian Book of the Dead discusses Egyptian philosophy on the process of death in detail. The elaborate preparation for death that the ancient Egyptians practiced was not because they had a fixation on death, but because they had an understanding of the eternality of the soul and of the many experiences accessible to the soul after death. Thus, it was wise to prepare and make arrangements for the living being as it moved from body to body [see chapter eight].

When the soul leaves the body, within twenty-four hours it is taken to a place where it experiences a certain amount of freedom for about a year of our time. After that period, the soul is brought for evaluation before a court headed by the superintendent of death. The court separates the pious activities from the impious and determines the degree to which that soul is to experience a peaceful, pleasant environment and the degree to which the soul is to be chastised and challenged in the next life. Souls may experience pleasure in the heavenly planets or pain in the hellish planets or they may also come to the middle, earthly planets which offer more of a balance of both.

It may take some souls thousands of lifetimes before they have the opportunity to come back to a physical form within this particular earthly atmosphere. The exact karmic requirements and arrangements that they need for their reentry may not be available—for example, the right parents or the proper physical environment. On the other hand, some people may have so many things to work out within an environment such as this earth that they are sent back immediately. At this time there are a lot of souls that have been waiting for long periods to reenter our atmosphere.

Abortions contribute to the backlog of suitable opportunities to take up another earthly body. As the number of abortions increase, the number of souls needing bodies increases. Thus, the length of time it takes for souls to reenter also increases. Because the astral plane is congested, the resulting energy over-flow and agitation are bombarding the general popu-lace here, causing an increase of chaos on the planet.

One may wonder whether it is at all possible to avoid this whole after-death procedure. Yes, it is. Sometimes a soul may have a very powerful connec-tion with an agent of the Supreme Lord, just as a wealthy man may have a powerful and well-known lawyer to represent him in a court of law. If the agent, such as a *guru*, is of a high quality, then sometimes the situation can be resolved without having to appear before the karmic board. This is usually the case if the soul is connected to the transcendental sys-tem and is no longer attached to the limitations of the material world.

Jesus and other prophets emphasized being *in* the world but not *of* the world. You are in this body now, but if you understand that this body is a garment, you won't get too caught up in identifying with and being attached to the body. Thus, when you leave your body, you will not have to be placed in a situation to work out your material attachments. God doesn't really chastise or reward you. He just arranges a situation in which you can work out that with which you are preoccupied. If you are preoccupied with functioning on the gross level like an animal, then you will receive a more suitable body for that activity. If you are attuned to exploiting people, you are going to find yourself in a situation where you will be able to experience what it is like to be exploited. If you are preoccupied with thoughts of divinity, spirituality, and transcendence, then your body is becoming spiritualized, and it is just a matter of time before you reach the spiritual dimension.

The Hellish Planets

Many of us are familiar with the old fire-and-brimstone preachers who are eternally forecasting the heated end to a sinful life. They warn that sinners are going to burn forever in a dark, hellish existence. This conception can lead to reluctance in worshiping a God who proposes to toss His children, parts of Himself, into a terrible furnace for eternity. Punishment, by definition, is a means of rectification, not annihilation. We would condemn any parents in society that treated their offspring so harshly as to kill them for a minor, or even a major, mistake. Why, then, do we accept such a harsh view of the God of love without challenge? Given God's loving nature, the concept of a hell in which we burn forever cannot be real. This is true even if we say that hell is controlled by the devil. Is the devil more powerful than God, such that God cannot reconnect with a soul that is in hell? The concept of hell is more complex than is dealt with normally. It is based on chastisement according to each individual's needs.

It is important to understand hell so that one can be equipped with knowledge to move as far away from it as possible. A child can be given positive encouragement by being shown positive things. Yet an understanding of what can happen if he or she approaches the negative can lead to more focused and thoughtful action. Knowledge of the hellish planets can bring about a necessary sense of fear so that one remains fortified by and focused on the Divine.

There are hundreds and thousands of hellish planets that the soul may have to visit. Although these are real in one sense, their existence is based on one's consciousness. Hell is in reality a mental concept and is experienced according to several variables. The experience is based on one's culture, one's religion, one's understanding, and one's consciousness. It is surely based on one's sins: the type, the quality, and extent of one's misdeeds. Animals do not go to hell. The animal's consciousness adapts and moves up to the next level automatically because the animal is not held accountable for its actions. Thus, an animal gets increasingly higher bodies until it reaches the human platform. Only at the human platform, where there is rational intelligence to pursue self-realization, is there accountability. It is in the human form that we are expected to understand our relationship of servitude to the Lord. The human body is an "escape body:" There is the greatest opportunity to escape the cycle of repeated birth and death while we are in this form. However, according to our actions, we may not be able to escape the reaction of the hellish planets. That will depend upon our consciousness.

In the hellish kingdoms, our desires become our greatest enemies. They bombard us and attack us and ultimately frustrate us because they cannot be fulfilled. Each hell is designed to accommodate different sinful activities. One who loves to torment and kill small creatures and lower entities has to pay the price of being attacked by the same type of creatures that one has abused or killed. The sensations of pain, misery, and torment are experienced over and over again because the soul does not die. Those that like to cook animals alive, such as dropping crabs, lobsters, and other marine crustaceans into boiling water just to satisfy the palate, will get to experience what that is like. They themselves will be dropped into a vat of boiling water, but they will not die. They will have to experience and endure such painful sensations again and again.

A special type of hell exists for administrators, kings, politicians, and government officials who commit extortion or who punish innocent people. Because they are in charge of many lives, there is a heavy penalty for misuse of their position. They will find themselves being crushed between two huge rollers just as easily as sugarcane is crushed to remove the juice. They will feel their internal organs being squashed and, again, they will not die. They will live through the painful experiences many, many times. Another kind of hell awaits those who indulge consistently in illicit sex that is not bound by the sanctity of marriage. They will be in an environment that is sexually surcharged and mental imagery will suggest that they are with the opposite sex. But they will realize they are actually embracing a red hot iron figure. They will suffer the burns and intolerable heat of that figure, but they will be unable to let go. They will experience this pain over and over again.

For alcoholics and drug addicts, there is a similar type of hell. Custodians of the hellish planet stand on their chests and pour molten lead down their throats. As in the other hells, the addicts do not die but must live and relive the torture repeatedly. Those who acquire money in an illegal or sinful way or who exploit, cheat, and connive without a sense of remorse have to experience their bodies being pierced by needles, just as a weaver pushes threads back and forth across a loom. A perpetual thief or robber will have skin removed bit by bit with red-hot iron tongs until the body is shredded to pieces. A man who forces a woman to engage in oral sex, with the intent of manipulating and controlling her, will find himself drowning in an ocean of semen, unable to find relief. A chronic liar will find his body constantly thrown off a high cliff and broken into pieces again and again.

Human sacrifice is unfortunately a popular practice in places around the world and it is growing in popularity here in America. In many cases, heads of state and fabulously rich people have obtained their power and riches by engaging in human sacrifice. They will have to undergo the rituals which they have forced on others. Their bodies are ripped apart by demonic beings who take great pleasure in drinking their blood and inflicting other nightmarish tortures upon them.

Although these souls are experiencing repeated suffering, the suffering is not eternal. God is not going to allow us to suffer forever because that would defeat the purpose of reformation. While a soul is undergoing the punishment, it simply feels as though the suffering will last for eternity. One of the most important aspects of going through the hellish environments is that an impression is left on the consciousness that makes it extremely uncomfortable to pursue that line of action again.

Sometimes impressions that have been imprinted on the subtle body from experiences in a previous life directly affect the present. Nightmares are sometimes due to a recollection of a visit to the hellish kingdoms. Someone may have a very intense phobia that has its roots in a previous life. Films we watch may trigger something in our consciousness that comes from experiences in other environments, such as the hellish planets. In many cases, people who are getting ready to leave the body (to die) may see entities from the hellish planets and become so frightened that they begin passing stool and urine or crying out for help. This occurs because according to our quality when we leave the body, we are given an initial experience which is reinforced later. That experience usually involves being escorted to the lower planets by agents of darkness (if we have been sinful) or to the upper planets or spiritual world by agents of light (if we have been pious).

Hell in Heaven

In the final category of hellish planets there is no torture. There are what are called subterranean heavenly planets. One may wonder why they are classified as hell. By definition, hell refers to how little God-consciousness there is. In the subterranean heavenly

planets there is an intense atmosphere of sense gratification and self-enjoyment, even to a greater extent
than in some of the higher heavenly planets. However,
there is little or no God-awareness. Certain types of
souls enter these planets and suffer there. It is like
being under house arrest. The environment seems
nice, but it is still a form of incarceration because the
souls are imprisoned by their desires to serve their
own senses instead of God. Attempts to serve the body,
mind, and senses rather than the Lord ultimately
result in misery.

These descriptions of the hellish planets sound
pretty far-fetched, but they are real for the beings
who need to experience them. For a person of higher
consciousness, such things do not exist. Each us of has
the ability to align ourselves with one reality or the
other. Once we have been exposed to this type of
information, our energy should be focused on how we
can reestablish our relationship with God, functioning in our natural role as His servants. The more our
desire to serve the Lord increases, the more provisions
are made so we never have to worry about these
material experiences again. Fear is natural, but the
power of love supersedes everything in this material
world. By raising our consciousness we can align ourselves with the source of all love and fulfill our purpose in this material arena without having to become
preoccupied with the rapidly decaying fabric of society or with the symptoms of an age coming to an end.

Question: If we know that we are suffering by not
surrendering to God, why is it so difficult to change

our behavior to avoid being aligned with a hellish consciousness?

Answer: Even though we may know that we are suffering from a hellish consciousness, it becomes difficult to change because of the influence of lust. As living entities, we are driven by lust. Lust is not limited to the arena of sexual interactions; it concerns all thoughts and actions focused on serving our senses. Lust is actually the reverse of love of God; it is a perverted reflection of love of God. It covers the consciousness of living entities in different degrees according to one's karmic patterns. The degree to which lust is covering a person determines how much that person will be dragged into a lower state of consciousness and brought down into a hellish condition.

We can become free from a hellish consciousness by giving up lust or, better still, by transforming that lust back into its original condition: unconditional love of God. This is done by the process of devotion. Some of the processes of devotion are: 1) hearing the name and glories of the Supreme Lord; 2) chanting His name and glories; 3) remembering the Lord; 4) serving the Lord; and 5) surrendering oneself fully to the Lord. Even though we are in this material world and it seems difficult to change our consciousness, it is possible to do so by aligning ourselves with devotional activities.

Question: My question concerns free will. I have heard many people say that if the Supreme ever made any mistake at all, it was giving free will to human beings. Would you explain why the Supreme has given us free will?

82

Answer: Love cannot be forced. By definition, love depends on an independent observation and evaluation and a willing interaction with another person. Because there is no imposition, a natural affection develops. Love is not someone holding a gun to your head and forcing you to say or do nice things. It is an activity of free will undertaken in a devotional mood, bringing forth loving energy and loving exchanges.

The Supreme Personality has given us free will to use in devotional service to Him. We are all sons and daughters of God but, unfortunately, we are often deviant sons and daughters. We are allowed free will to choose either to serve God or to try to be separate from God—at least temporarily. We say "temporarily" because this is only an artificial separation, one which must come to an end. We can never be really separate from the Lord, but we can choose to use our free will to run away from Him. We are given that much leeway. When a child is deviant and causes the mother some difficulty, the mother may say, "Just go to your room and do what you like." Although the child is in the room, the mother is still concerned and still wishes the best for the child. But due to the child's insistence on learning through experience, instead of learning through hearing, the parent says, "Okay, just do what you like," giving the child the freedom to play out his or her desires. Although they never take away the child's free will, parents try to do what is best for the child. They educate the child so that he or she can use that free will properly in due course.

That scenario is basically what our situation is like here in the material world. We are being given some leeway to use our free will, and we generally use it in the wrong way. But as soon as we want to turn back or as soon as we grow tired of trying to experience enjoyment outside of our connection with the Lord, then we are on our way back home to God. In the learning process, many times we are faced with severe difficulties. We may have to go through multiple lifetimes of hardship, until we are no longer satisfied with the mundane, until we strive for what is rightfully ours: love of God. When we become even a little bit aware of this, we start to investigate the meaning of life more seriously. As soon as we start this exploration, help is available. The Lord sends us highly evolved souls, the scriptures, and divine insight as support as we advance toward Him.

Question: Based on my religious upbringing, I grew up with a lot of fear about going to hell if I was bad. In spiritual life is it necessary to fear God or to even have fear? Isn't the power of love stronger?

Answer: The power of love is the strongest force in creation. When it is not properly directed, however, it becomes one of the most devastating forces because it becomes a force of lust and greed. Lust and love are different sides of the same coin, just as electricity can be used to heat or cool things depending on how it is channeled. It is lust that causes so much of man's inhumanity to man. It causes so much abuse, misuse and exploitation. It is love that has the ability to rectify and heal.

An immature child has conditioned responses based on rewards and punishments. Punishments instill fear, but as the child matures, behavior is based on love. Thus, the child thinks, "Mommy and Daddy will be disturbed if I do this; so I will not do it." When the love is not so grounded, the child thinks, "I must not do this, because if I do, I will get punished."

Similarly, when our spirituality is not very deep, our relationship with the Supreme Lord is based on rewards, punishment and fear. We don't behave in certain ways because we don't want to be chastised. As we mature, our choices to act or not act are no longer based on fear. Instead, they are determined by our willingness to render selfless service and we become eager to do what is required out of genuine love. As the surrender becomes deep and sincere, the Lord reciprocates with blessings and grace accordingly. Ultimately, everything is based on our surrender and devotion.

The major fear that people experience is fear about the future. Actually, there is nothing but the present. The past is already gone; its traits and patterns are upon us now. The future is just around the corner; it is becoming the present moment by moment. If we were more conscious about the present, we wouldn't be so fearful about the future, especially because we would have more control of what form that future would take. What we do now prepares for us what we will receive in the future. This is *karma*. Our present thoughts and activities produce certain future reactions. The people who are most fearful are those who are the most insecure. Those who are insecure should take a closer look at their belief systems and lifestyles.

Sometimes people are fearful because they are afraid of what someone is going to do to them or of what they are doing to themselves. Sometimes people are fearful about what they have done or are doing to others. People are also fearful because their life circumstances are not as focused or stable as they would like.

The presence of fear indicates that there is a poor quality of love in our lives, a weakness in our relationship with God. This brings about suffering, and with suffering there is pain. When we feel pain, we should try to accept it and use its energy to move us forward. How we perceive the world around us greatly influences our degree of frustration and misery. It is important to learn how to make negative situations positive and positive events even more positive. It is especially critical to make negative circumstances positive because our environment is already negative and hostile. The message in the environment is that our identity is material rather than spiritual. We are taught to be sexist, racist, and sectarian. We are taught that we should beg, borrow, steal or do whatever we can to "get ours" without any concern about the future or about who gets hurt in the process. This philosophy permeates today's society.

Since we are not going to be able to avoid negativity totally, it is best to learn how to coexist with it and use it as a stepping stone. When one is walking up a flight of stairs, each step can be a struggle, especially if there are obstacles; each step can be seen as a confrontation. Yet, as we step up each one anyway, we increase our sense of achievement and growth. Similarly, negativity can be used as a stepping stone for accelerated growth. If it is not used in this way, spiritual advancement will be very difficult.

Whatever your situation, say to yourself, "How can I learn from this situation? For some reason it has come before me. Since the Lord is my well-wisher and is merciful, magnanimous, and greatly concerned about my welfare, this situation is occurring for my own betterment, for my own growth. The Lord is giving me a test to see if I am able to pass it." A teacher gives tests to determine how well the student has internalized a given lesson. The results of the test indicate the student's mastery of the material. The teacher does not give students tests to set them up for failure, but to assess progress. Similarly, the Lord does not want us to fail. The Lord tests us to clarify our level of spiritual development and to challenge us to grow. So, in every situation, ask yourself: "How can I use this situation to increase my loving understanding, sentiments and reactions?" If you do this, every situation will bring about growth and progress.

The way that we view positive events is also important. When something positive happens, if we feel that it was due us and question why God took so long to bring it about, we are not practicing the proper consciousness of gratitude. However, if we properly use what we have and accept any additions or improvements with the attitude that we are not really worthy yet we are thankful for what the Lord has sent, then there will be spiritual progress. When positive circumstances come, use them in a consciousness of gratitude and appreciation. In the same way, when negative situations come, use them to gain strength and fortitude.

Obviously, this is easier said than done. But every action stems from a thought or reflection. If you believe something is possible and if you seriously attempt to bring the situation about, it can become a reality. However, if you don't even consider the possibilities and don't try, the potential for success is limited, to say the least. So, always remember that our consciousness can decrease suffering. Have you ever noticed that there are certain people who, even if exposed to a contagious disease, don't get infected? And when such people do become ill, they are able to restore their bodies to health very quickly. While they are sick, their spirits are high and they don't even look like they are sick. This occurs because they do not affirm sickness through their thought patterns. Their consciousness is one of health and well-being. Changing our consciousness can be a powerful painkiller and lead to quick recovery.

As children of God, we want to act in harmony with God's will because of our love for Him. Fear can be healthy when it is directed towards those things that can take us away from the Lord. We should fear the whole material world because it represents the alternative to serving God. It is wise to maintain a healthy paranoia about the pull that the material energy exerts upon us. We should always be on our guard, knowing that at any moment we can become casualties of war. This type of fear is healthy because it motivates us to be strong spiritual warriors; it pushes us towards increasing our love of and service to the Lord.

5
Psychic Intrusion

This is an unusual time on the planet because most people are prisoners; they are not able to exercise their own free will. The mental space of most people on this planet is being intruded upon and their minds are being controlled by an overload of negative energy. Mental and spiritual incarceration is a normal state of affairs and there is a tremendous abuse of psychic knowledge.

History shows us that there have always been serious consequences for the misuse of higher knowledge. Such behavior has resulted in the disappearance of highly advanced cultures and the destruction of civilizations. Unless the present misuse of knowledge is stopped and our energies are positively redirected, we will not have a viable future on this planet.

Limited Senses

Consider the limited nature of the human condition. The human body itself has many limitations. Our senses do not tell us the truth; they lie to us at every moment. Our ears and eyes are not as acute as we might think. We cannot hear the sounds nor see the sights that occur merely one building away. Sometimes we're not even aware of what's going on right under our nose. We can only perceive certain phenomena through the use of microscopes, telescopes, or other types of amplifying equipment. Otherwise, we're virtually helpless. We can't smell an odor from the back of the room and sometimes we can't smell things that are only a few feet away! We are not consciously aware of the clothes touching our bodies. The range of what we perceive as reality is in actuality incredibly narrow. Events occur all around us that are beyond our immediate awareness; a whole imperceptible realm exists that has direct effects on us. Given these facts, it easy to understand how we can be psychically controlled.

Subliminal Suggestion

One popular method of mind control is subliminal suggestion. This can be defined as the process of introducing information at a level below the threshold of conscious awareness, in an attempt to direct the course of one's thoughts or actions. Although it occurs surreptitiously, most people are aware that it is widely used—especially in advertising. Advertisements in magazines, in newspapers, on billboards or on television are designed to affect the subconscious through the use of various kinds of imagery, often of a sexual nature. The sexual overtones link the advertised product to pleasure, and it is this anticipation of a pleasurable experience that stimulates a desire for the product.

As masters of psychology, advertisers frequently create an illusion of need for superfluous items. Driven by the senses, the consumer becomes a puppet easily manipulated by the media. In one study, viewers in a movie theater were given subliminal messages during the movie to buy a specific soft drink. They proved the effectiveness of the messages by buying more of that particular drink during the movie than of any other product.

Because of television's broad and dedicated audience, television advertisements are particularly effective. Millions of people regularly watch the same show and the same advertisements at the same time each day. With satellite technology, a program can be presented around the world, reaching millions. The effectiveness of television advertising is one of the reasons it is so expensive. Thousands of dollars for a few seconds of advertising is not uncommon. Only the giants of the business world can afford the astronomical fees. They pay them in an attempt to make their own personal agenda the dominant one—an agenda that generally begins with money and power and often ends in control and exploitation.

The hypnotic nature of television is another contributing factor to the great influence of this medium. Your normal waking consciousness is called the "beta" state. When you watch television, on the other hand, you enter what is called an "alpha" state; the brain is more calm, relaxed and meditative. You must be extremely careful in this alpha state because you are inordinately receptive to incoming information, rather like a sponge soaking up a liquid. In a normal conversation, you evaluate what is being said. You are able to be on guard and decide whether you are going to accept or reject the ideas that are being offered. However, you typically watch television at home, in your best chair or on your most comfortable couch, eating your favorite snack. You are relaxed. You're in a very pleasing environment and, therefore, more passive than usual while all sorts of ideas are being programmed into you. Essentially, television provides a very effective form of hypnosis.

You have probably noticed how difficult it is to get the attention of someone who is watching television. Even when you call the person's name, it takes awhile for that individual to be jolted out of the intoxicated state. Even if one just walks by a television with no plans to look at it, it is easy to be drawn towards it. Television has that degree of powerful effect.

An experiment was conducted in California in which five-and six-year-old children were asked the following question: "Who do you like the best: daddy or television?" The majority of the children preferred television! The average person experiences a great amount of pleasure through television and spends a great many hours per day watching it. Because of the dominant themes of violence, exploitation, and perversion, children as well as adults are being given negative messages about life's goals and the means to attain them.

Power in Music

Another way to manipulate the consciousness is by infusing the ethers with polluting sound vibrations, particularly through music. This is a very powerful means of control because sound affects human consciousness at the deepest possible level. Subliminal messages through the medium of music provide a means of psychic control. The self-development movement makes use of tapes with subliminal messages to assist people with their growth. However, negative messages can be given just as easily as positive ones. Although the conscious mind may be unaware of the messages, the subconscious mind is being programmed. Supermarkets and department stores use subliminal messages to boost sales. Hidden in the canned Muzak is often a message to purchase a particular set of items. Stores also use these messages in a positive way. Experiments indicate that subtle suggestions not to steal have decreased the amount of shoplifting significantly. By constantly projecting these sounds, the store owners have saved millions of dollars.

We can see the power of sound vibration in the effects of certain types of music. There is music that increases aggression. There is music that stimulates the base emotions of lust, selfishness, and violence. At concerts where passionate rock music is performed, there is a higher likelihood of drug use, sex, and even violence. Soft instrumental music, on the other hand, promotes a mood of peace and happiness.

To look at the power of sound from another angle, people who take care of plants know that the growth of plants is affected not only by soil, water and light, but also by the people and sounds in the environment. Research has shown that certain rock **music** stunts the growth of plants, and in some cases, **kills** them. Such sound vibrations affect various parts of the body of plants no less than that of humans and animals. Different sound vibrations stimulate different *chakras* in the body. Rock music tends to stimulate the lower chakras. Studies have shown that students who listen to certain rock music while studying achieve lower grades and are less productive.

Some musicians and entertainers have advertised the fact that they have direct links with satanic cults. Their records often sympathize with demonic entities, use demonic symbols, and some records, if played backwards, directly worship Satan. Violence, perversion, and exploitation are always involved in satanic rituals. Because power comes from these rituals, people make contracts with lower entities in order to develop untold powers. Demonic consciousness produces negative vibrations. The more chaotic the energy, the more strength it gives the demons. Some performers have been known to bite off the heads of chickens and bats, and some to drink the blood of animals on stage. This is obviously abnormal, demonic activity.

Suggestion by Remote Control

Neuro-linguistic programming (NLP) is a means by which one can stimulate certain responses in others and interpret others' behavior. One method is to examine people's eye movements as they are questioned. If they look up and to the left, they are said to be visualizing something that they have seen in the past. If they look to the left but on a horizontal level, they are remembering something they have heard in the past. These patterns are said to be usually exhibited by right-handed people. The patterns are reversed for some left-handed individuals. Another technique involves varying the pace and rate of your speech to influence the listener's interpretation of what is being said.

Body movements are used also to stimulate the brain. There are two major parts of the brain: the left hemisphere, which controls the rational, objective, and materialistic functions, and the right hemisphere, which controls the subjective, intuitive, mystical, and spiritual ones. By moving your left hand, for example, you can stimulate right-brain activity in another person. All of these NLP techniques can be used to direct people's energy. In fact, many government officials, lawyers, politicians, and top business administrators are trained in the interpretation of body language, use of speech and hand movements.

Are Your Thoughts Your Own?

Often people's moods do not originate with themselves, but are suggestions projected into their mental space by others. This is done unconsciously for the most part by one person onto another or by groups of people to each other. In some cases, however, thoughts are deliberately projected in someone's direction to stop or direct particular cognitive, emotive, or behavioral patterns.

We all utilize some of these mind-control techniques knowingly or unknowingly. Some people have adopted these techniques without even consciously knowing why or how they work; they just know that they work. Along these same lines, people often use visualization techniques to attain specific goals.

A very effective technique used by politicians and salespersons is the technique of disorientation. It's interesting to see how this works: physically, if you slip and you're about to fall, the tendency is to grab anything you can to regain your stability. Similarly, when you are insecure in your life and mentally faltering, you naturally grab for something that you hope will reestablish your sense of equilibrium. If someone is there reaching out, ready to put something in your hand, you will take it. If you do not happen to be in a state of insecurity or vulnerability, the manipulator will create such a state, and then offer whatever it is he or she wants you to have or believe. For example, an insurance salesperson might have you visualize your home on fire or a terrible accident and then introduce solutions for you to grab onto. Politicians often use the "yes, yes, yes" strategy. For example, someone running for office stands at the podium and carries on this exchange with the audience:

> "Oh citizens of this wonderful city, I'm sure you're all tired of the bad roads."
> > "Yes!"
> "You're tired of pollution."
> > "Yes!"
> "You're tired of drugs."
> > "Yes!"
> "So please vote for me . . . "
> > "Yes!"

The implanted idea is that if you elect John Doe, all the problems he mentioned will be solved. Stimulated by the rhythm that was created, you opened yourself up to being programmed in a particular way.

We experience such situations on one level or another every day. At times we are conscious of what is happening, yet there is still so much of which we are unaware.

Psychics at Work

A psychic is a person who is especially attuned and sensitive to energies beyond the physical realm. Psychics can use their abilities positively, to assist others, or negatively, as a means of controlling others. They can, from a separate room, literally put someone to sleep and then revive that individual, who has no awareness of the intrusion. In documented cases, some psychics have focused their energies on a person's nervous system and overwhelmed it, administering a psychic knockout! Everyone has the ability to develop these faculties. Some have developed them more than others to the point where they can influence someone's thoughts or see what another is doing in a distant place.

Many world leaders, today as well as in the past, are involved in some of these pursuits. Hitler explored psychic phenomena. It is believed that Napoleon was a psychic. Stalin interacted with a very powerful psychic, Wolf Messing, instructing him to rob a bank. The psychic handed a blank note to the bank teller and mentally willed him to hand over a sum of money. He intruded upon the teller's mental space to such a degree that the teller promptly handed over the money.

Much research has been conducted on psychic phenomena and continues to this day. The former Soviet Union has invested millions of dollars in their best institutions for training psychics and has done fascinating experiments with subtle powers. America, too, has invested much time, money, and manpower in the military uses of psychic energy. Great amounts of money and the most sophisticated technology are being used in the areas of espionage. If intelligence specialists really want to discover something, they have the ability to do so. Practically any electrical appliance in your home can be used to gather information about you.

In the world today, there is an increasing polarization between those who are focused on manipulation and exploitation and those focused on spiritual growth and inner development. We are in the midst of a war—not a physical war but a war for the control of our minds. This subtle warfare is much more serious than any external war of physical confrontation. This mental war is far more intense and insidious.

The world is at its worst and best right now. It is in its worst state because everything is in disarray. There is little stability politically, economically, or sociologically. The government's ability to control is crumbling. There is an impending economic crisis, and political underhandedness is at an all-time high. It is a period of great unrest and danger. Many countries have stockpiles of chemical and nuclear weapons, and like frightened children, their nervousness and fear can manifest in widespread destruction. This is the best of times because it is a period in which to assess our spiritual growth and make great progress if we desire. Everything is available at this juncture to allow us to become fully dependent on the Lord.

Techniques for Psychic Defense and Fortification

The focus of psychic defense is not to impart warfare, but to teach you certain protective strategies to enable you to remain the free spirit that you are. The key is self-realization. This means you must work on yourself. Any teacher can stimulate you, but there must be an underlying desire and commitment on your part to raise your consciousness. Five points will be presented here for your consideration.

Point One

The more you identify with your mind, the more you can become susceptible to mind intrusion. Although you have been conditioned to see your mind as you, your mind is actually not you. You are the user of the mind in the same way that you are the user of your shoes, your coat, or your sweater; you are the person who makes use of your mind. Whatever you use is not you. It is actually the soul that uses the intellect, the mind, and the body.

The mind is constantly engaged in accepting and rejecting stimuli in its environment. Your environment, particularly your immediate environment, largely determines what your mind grabs and holds onto. In most cases, the mind is your worst enemy, because your mind has been conditioned to tell you that you should go after whatever your senses desire. Your mind has been conditioned to tell you that as long as you are identifying with the basic functions of eating, sleeping, mating, and defending, then there is nothing else to worry about. The "you" that the mind tells you to be is not the real you.

There is a greater you, a greater potential within yourself, within the soul. So how do you handle the mind? A powerful technique is to treat your mind as another person who is speaking to you. When your mind starts telling you things that are unhealthy or untrue, when your mind starts giving you grief, when your mind starts causing fear, when your mind starts arousing anxiety, don't accept these thoughts. You can better reject them if you have already realized that there is a distinction between the mind and you. Always remember that because you are separate from the mind, you can evaluate what the mind is dictating to you.

This practice will help you when you are the target of mind intrusion and are not really responsible for the mental energy that is being imposed upon you. You will act with wisdom because you will be able to recognize what is occurring.

As long as you identify with the mind, you immediately act upon what the mind dictates. The mind will control you, instead of the opposite, and will cause needless complications. You must constantly evaluate what is going in and coming out of the mind. Someone who is thinking of you is entering into your mental space. In most cases, people are not thinking loving thoughts about each other. If you are spiritually advanced and have enviable qualities, you are particularly at risk. All kinds of people thinking envious thoughts can make you a target of lust and exploitation. It is as if they are feeding on you. You really have no idea of all the thoughts, the energy, or the life forms that you are carrying around with you. Your consciousness will determine which concerns will be the dominant ones that you hold onto and accept. Much of your reality is based on how you codify things. Don't accept your thoughts as if they were the truth. Otherwise the mind is going to enslave you.

Point Two

It is important to not identify with your own or others' problems. When people tell you their problems, they literally give these difficulties to you. You are now carrying their problems, and usually their problems continue to increase because they are thinking of nothing else. You may also find yourself so overwhelmed by your own challenges that you feel like you are under a great weight and are unable to move. A little technique in dealing with these situations is to visualize yourself the way you want to be when you have reached a state of perfection or have moved to a higher level. As you focus on that image, you are creating it and you will bring yourself back up again.

Point Three

Because the state of the body has a powerful effect on consciousness, your diet is a vital weapon of psychic defense. You have to create higher energy in order to not be affected by the lower energy. If you are making your body a graveyard by eating meat, it will be very difficult to eliminate negative forces from your life. If you're taking a corpse into your body, you are making your body a cemetery for dead animals. A psychic looking at a graveyard sees all kinds of disembodied spirits. People who live near graveyards are often bombarded with psychological problems because of the energy that is located there. Imagine the effects of constantly making your body a graveyard by eating dead flesh. Consider how meat decays in the open and what it is doing in your body. If you study vegetarianism you will see that nutritionally, morally, ethically, and spiritually, vegetarianism is a preferred diet for a saner society.

Point Four

Intoxication, in all its forms and to any degree, makes us very vulnerable to psychic intrusion. You've heard alcoholics talk about seeing pink elephants. This is not a hallucination. As you allow your body to degenerate under the effects of intoxication, the vibration of the body moves into lower planes of existence. As you tune into these lower planes, you contact disembodied beings.

It is no accident that much of the world is now suffering from drug-related problems. Worldwide infrastructures will continue to fall apart as long as those who run them remain addicted to drugs. Metaphysically, if you take drugs you are putting holes in your astral body. It is as if you were summoning the entities associated with psychic intrusions, mental attacks, and possessions. Most people who take drugs have a visitor inside of them of whom they are totally unaware. They have much more than just the drug hindering them; they are carrying various beings with them. Some of these entities just wait for opportunities and environments where they can intrude. If you are opening your door and calling, then somebody might come in. Using drugs is like "calling in" unwanted subtle visitors.

In addition to drugs and alcohol, gambling is another form of intoxication. In places such as Las Vegas and Atlantic City, people become addicted to getting something for nothing. Because there are clearly defined symptoms in people who are addicted to gambling, it is now viewed as a distinct disease. People are treated in clinics because they can't control themselves. Lottery systems are not in place by accident. The state lottery systems are "bail-out" mechanisms used when a state is in financial trouble. Leaders are fully aware that gambling is a form of intoxication and can result in much financial gain. One involved in gambling is also opening the door and inviting outside entities in.

Point Five

The proper use of sexual energy is critical for inner stabilization and psychic protection. One of the highest uses of sexual energy is to attract pious souls to take birth in this realm, offering them a commitment to spiritually guide and nurture them. In this way, these souls will eventually take up the role of guides and teachers themselves. Utter misuse of sexual energy can be seen in practices such as pornography.

Pornography totally devalues the beauty of the male-female relationship. It directs men to view women as pleasure units to be manipulated and enjoyed. Pornography propagates a mentality of irresponsibility and produces minds that are controlled by perversion. Pornography is very lucrative through means such as magazines and the film and recording industries. Along with drugs, it is one of the biggest and fastest-growing industries on the planet. It has now reached the point that many children are being abducted for pornographic films and satanic rituals. We are surrounded everywhere with these types of negative energy.

To ultimately minimize the effects of the psychic bombardment that surrounds us all, you can follow the model of martial arts. In martial arts you don't necessarily have to confront an attack with a counter-attack. Instead, you can get behind the enemy or side-step him so that you move yourself out of the way of his or her energy. You don't have to feed into it. You can transcend it. You do this by first analyzing yourself in those areas just mentioned: controlling the mind, positive thinking, healthy diet, avoiding intoxication, and proper use of sexual energy. This self-examination process will automatically make you stronger. You will create more protection for yourself just by contemplating your situation. Thus, you don't have to worry about all the various types of psychic attack that may be occurring; you will naturally have a field of protection around you due to your fortified consciousness. Love, righteousness, and the Divine are stronger than the negativity of this age. Therefore, be loving and righteous. The more you align with the

Divinity, the more protection you will have and the greater will be your spiritual advancement.

Question: How can we extend love to others, yet at the same time protect ourselves from taking in unhealthy energy?

Answer: We should try to see everyone as an energy of God—our friend as well as our enemy, our supporter as well as our attacker. It doesn't mean that when you see a tiger, you put your head in the tiger's mouth because you love everyone. Nor does it mean that you automatically accept any type of behavior. You can hate the sin and love the sinner.

Some people are less aware than others of their potential divinity, of their inherent nature as spiritual beings. Thus, they are captured by a strong sense of materialism or negativity. If this is understood, there is less desire to attack when someone is attacking you. If you allow yourself to get on the same level of energy as one who is absorbed in negativity, then you lose. Again, the technique is the same as in martial arts. You don't attack with the same energy; instead, you step behind or to the side, and use the person's energy in a way that helps the situation. As we experience real concern about the person, then we transmit some of that love into the individual. The individual will then be upgraded or will be so determined to hold onto a position that at least he or she will avoid you. For example, if you know someone who has a very negative outlook on life, whenever that person comes near you, instead of talking about problems, talk about something of a higher nature. The person will then realize that in order to associate with you, he or she has to rise to your level.

Another point is that the more spiritually developed you become, the higher your energy will be. You should give your association to others but not accept the attitudes of a lower-energy person. The way you do that is to keep a constant barrier against the negativity that a person is projecting. Although you love that person, you know that in order to be of help you must keep yourself spiritually fit. Otherwise, you can't help the other person or yourself.

Relationships just based on sentiment rather than growth bring degradation to all involved. You must commit not to participate in negativity nor encourage creation of more negativity, so that you will not become wounded or become a casualty. By associating in a way that is giving rather than accepting, you are protecting yourself and the other person also. If there is an attack, you forgive, but you also want to make sure that the person gets some help to deal with the sickness. If you can't help the sickness, at least you can keep yourself from becoming sick. The only way to do this is to stay focused by maintaining spiritually elevated thoughts. You cannot allow yourself to be devastated by the negative. Rather, you must learn the art of transforming the negative into the positive.

Question: You mentioned that the mind can be our enemy. How are we to divorce ourselves from our minds and see the mind as a different person? First, how do I define myself as myself without the mind, and second, how can I separate the mind from the intelligence?

Answer: Let's look at our biological hierarchy. First, we have the body and the senses. Higher than these is the mind. Higher than the mind is the intelligence. Higher than the intelligence is the soul. Let's consider how these various levels interrelate. The senses respond to the sense objects in the immediate environment. The senses give a command to the mind to do something to gratify them. The intelligence usually has a more ethical, moral orientation. It tells the mind, "But if you do that, then this will be the consequence," or "Do it this way. Don't do that." By keeping ourselves immersed in spiritual or transcendental knowledge—subjects that are not just material but about higher growth and love of God—then the intelligence is sharpened. It can keep the mind in check because it engages the mind in higher-order activities. Then the mind will be less influenced by lower-order preoccupations.

The main point is that we don't have to accept everything that comes into our mental environment. Just assess the thoughts as you would assess a person who comes into your presence. You know whether the person is coming to harass you, to ask for something, or just to be with you. Let's say someone walks up to you. At first, you're likely to be a little skeptical. You'll quickly want to assess the nature of this encounter. Similarly, when the mind comes to you, check it out, evaluate it, and qualify it. Don't just accept whatever it brings to you, because the mind has been conditioned to keep you in a state of illusion.

Question: How do you know when you are dealing with a true psychic?

Answer: To understand psychics, one should first understand something about the psychic realm, the realm that deals with paranormal experiences. There are a variety of psychic phenomena and abilities. One category of psychic phenomena involves having experiences beyond the gross physical senses, such as in remote viewing. Remote viewing is the ability to perceive what is going on in another location. It can be likened to the ability to send your eyes and mind somewhere else while your body remains where it is. You can then observe a situation and report what is occurring. Another psychic ability is clairaudience, which means that you can hear something that is not in your immediate environment. This may involve hearing or seeing realities in other dimensions.

Another category of psychic phenomena is mental telepathy, which refers to receiving impressions with the mind, as in reading someone else's thoughts. Two other areas are hypnosis, the ability to induce a state of heightened susceptibility to suggestion, and psychokinesis, which is the use of mental energy to move objects. There are other types of psychic abilities along these same lines.

There is another classification of abilities known as *siddhis*; this literally means "mystic perfections." The *siddhi* known as *anima* is the ability to become very small, like a particle. *Kamavasayita-siddhi* is the ability to assume any shape or form one desires. *Prapti-siddhi* is a mystic power that enables one to acquire a material

item from any place in the universe without physically going to get it. The ability to control all the
material elements is *vasitva-siddhi*.

There is a certain *siddhi* that allows one to summon
the soul of a person who has just died back into the
physical body. Jesus Christ, Ezekiel, and Elijah in the
Christian tradition were able to revive people from the
dead. Since the physical body is just a garment, the
soul has the ability to come and go. Thus, someone
who has developed this particular mystic perfection
can summon a soul back into the body.

In our current day and age, many people visit psychics and channelers and involve themselves in various
types of *yogas*. But they often confuse the "psychic"
with the "spiritual." Much of what people perceive to
be spiritual is usually something that is of the subtle
material realm. Someone who witnesses a miracle usually assumes that something divine has occurred. This
is not necessarily the case. These events can just be a
matter of knowing how to use certain laws and how to
convert certain types of energies.

Energy has two polarities: positive and negative.
You can use the negative polarity to invoke power from
disembodied or sinful entities. Sometimes a person can
become possessed and perform a variety of unusual
feats that are not of a God-centered nature. Much of
the channeling involves connections from the astral
plane, which is nothing more than a subtle dimension
just a bit above the gross material level; it is not from
the anti-material, or spiritual, plane. It often is not of
a divine origin. Sometimes the messages come from
disembodied beings on a gross, sinful or dangerous
platform, while at other times the messages are just

metaphysical gymnastics. These malevolent entities will cause people to think that a "mystical" experience is something spiritual when in actuality it is not. The entities will then exploit people. Such exploitation is quite common in the field of metaphysics.

Many people are involved in metaphysical and spiritual organizations. It is important to be able to draw the line of demarcation between the metaphysical and the spiritual. If a person displays mystic powers but does not have a loving orientation, we should immediately be cautious. Individuals engaged in illicit affairs, intoxication, gambling or meat-eating cannot contact higher spiritual planes. If we seek out such people expecting their knowledge to be very high, we may in fact find that their body is terribly contaminated. If we associate with them, we are taking a tremendous risk. God is not so cheap or weak that He has to speak through such contaminated vehicles.

Excessive fascination with metaphysical phenomena can hinder spiritual advancement. For one truly striving to grow spiritually, these are nothing more than interferences. They are pitfalls that often decrease the chance of making spiritual advancement toward the real goal of becoming a loving servant of the Supreme Personality of Godhead, the Supreme Lord. Preoccupation with these phenomena is not a sign of advancement. There are planets where all the residents have many of the mystic powers we have enumerated and for them it is no great accomplishment [see chapter two]. For entities of some of the lower realms, our psychic experiences would seem to demonstrate great advancement, when to us they are just part of our day-to-day lives. Just as a primitive person would find it amazing to see someone use a calculator, entities of the lower realms are astounded by some routine things that we take for granted. In other words, what is mystical for one is commonplace for another. It's all relative. When you understand this, you see that often what we call psychic or mystic is simply a matter of something unusual or unorthodox, something different from the normally accepted scheme of activities. But that's all. It might seem mystical to you for someone to pull up the hood of his car and immediately solve a mechanical problem. However, that individual has simply acquired a certain level of knowledge that is unavailable to you. Thus, if we are too fascinated by the gross material level or even the subtle material level, we become stagnated.

Many spiritualists aspiring for the highest goal of love of God such as *rishis* (great Vedic scholars) and *yogis* (those who practice connecting with God through one of the disciplines of *yoga*), often fall down when they acquire some of these powers. This is because these powers give one the ability to manipulate the material energy, and such powers can become intoxicating. People who have these abilities can feel that they are the ultimate controllers of everything, which can be a very serious problem.

We have taken birth in this material world because we are envious of the Supreme, because we want to be God. We can see around us how people are trying to be the most renounced, the most beautiful, the most knowledgeable, or the most wealthy. These opulences belong to the Supreme, yet humans make herculean efforts to become the supreme possessors of these qualities. If we want to be released from these entanglements, to acquire liberation and, ultimately, to have divine personal association with the Supreme Godhead, we must become free from all of these contaminations. When we are too fascinated with psychic manipulation or the activities of the subtle material plane, we become more and more bound to the material world and are kept lifetime after lifetime in this mundane sphere. What is necessary is to find a lover of God, not a psychic.

6
UFOs, Extraterrestrials, and the Mother-ship

*U*nidentified flying objects (UFOs), extraterrestrials and the mother-ship are topics that conventional thinkers have historically regarded as disreputable or, at best, questionable. However, the large number of reports and photographic records of these phenomena indicate that they merit serious consideration. These phenomena are real, and this discussion will explore them at some length. While those who have a foundation in metaphysical subjects will have a fuller understanding and appreciation of the subject matter, all can benefit from exposure to these topics.

Finding the Future in the Past

A broad definition of extraterrestrials, or aliens, is that they are entities who reside beyond the boundaries of the earth planet. This includes beings from the planetary systems higher than earth—demigods—and those beings from planetary systems lower than the earth.

All ancient cultures have had extraterrestrial involvement at one level or another. Many civilizations left oral histories and writings of extraterrestrial entities. The Native American, African, Latin and South American peoples, among others, have passed many stories down from generation to generation about extraterrestrial contacts. The history of Kemet (Egypt) suggests that the pyramids may have been built with the help of extraterrestrials. These beings were instrumental in imparting knowledge about lasers and other technology that was passed down through a select group of people to be used in particular ways. The pyramids were not really designed as tombs. Instead, one of their functions was that of amplifiers to aid in communication between different dimensions, allowing entities to be in tune with some of their brothers and sisters in other realms [see chapter eight].

You Mean That's in the Scriptures?

The scriptures speak of extraterrestrials, although in some scriptures the information is obscured by cryptic language. In the Bible, the chapter of Ezekiel mentions how Ezekiel saw a "wheel" and that the wheel picked him up and took him to a higher wheel. Some suggest that this higher wheel refers to a heavenly ship. The book of Revelations indicates that as the world approaches a state of transition, a city will appear in the heavens. Both of these references refer to a special kind of UFO called a mother-ship, which will be described later. A Christian minister named Barry Downing has written extensively about the Bible and UFO phenomena.

The Vedic scriptures of India like the Bhagavata Purana, the Mahabharata and the Ramayana describe in detail beings from other planetary systems; the aerial vehicles, or *vimanas*, in which they travel; and their ongoing contact with humans.

The Mother-ship

A term frequently heard in UFO discussions is *mother-ship*. A mother-ship is a type of UFO that is like a huge "flying city." A mother-ship can contain hundreds or even thousands of smaller ships that are the size of ballrooms. If fully lit up, a mother-ship would shine more powerful than 10,000 suns. They are incredibly large.

There have been times in our history when mother-ships have appeared, but the occurrences were misunderstood. For example, the Star of Bethlehem was a mother-ship. The destruction of the cities of Sodom and Gomorrah was carried out by a mother-ship. Angel Gabriel and Moses had connections with a mother-ship. Many of the Vedic *vimanas* were mother-ships. Several years ago, a Japanese pilot reported a strange sighting: he was being followed by fifty to sixty small units coming out of a larger unit. This was a mother-ship as well.

The beings of the mother-ships look more like us than any other extraterrestrial being. They have always monitored this particular universe. Their role is to assist the earth with balance and advancement.

They are providing support through the transformation of consciousness that is happening now and the transformation that will be necessary in the future. They are able to prevent certain catastrophes and currently are monitoring nuclear armaments to help control this precarious situation.

History has recorded the continuous battle between good and evil, both of which fight to control the fate of humankind. As beings of higher consciousness (and those striving to attain a higher consciousness) come increasingly in contact with those who still seek selfish gain, a phenomenal cleansing takes place. Life on the planet is partially or completely destroyed. Mother-ships are responsible for ensuring that the population is reestablished after this cleansing. During destructive events, beings of the mother-ship "beam up" human beings of high levels of consciousness. This pick-up is by a beam of light and happens instantaneously, as fast as thought. The humans who are picked up are put to sleep immediately, especially if the circumstances under which they were picked up are extremely serious, such as in a catastrophe requiring global evacuation. These people will help to reseed the planet at a later time. Those whose bodies are destroyed are those who have not surrendered to the Supreme. They actually benefit from the destruction because, since they were not able to advance spiritually in that life, they will receive another opportunity to advance in a new lifetime.

Beings from mother-ships do not directly function in the world of human beings. Most of their work has to be done indirectly through the beings on the earth plane. Because we always have free will to make our own choices with the concomitant consequences, they offer guidance to earthlings who then are free to choose a particular course of action.

The Nation of Islam and the Mother-ship

The Honorable Elijah Muhammad, in his book *Message to the Blackman in America*, and Minister Louis Farrakhan, both of the Nation of Islam, make reference to mother-ships. *Message to the Blackman* mentions the mother-ship's role and its ability to keep this world on an even keel by activities such as controlling disasters, natural and man-made.

Some years ago, Minister Farrakhan shared an experience he had that was similar to the biblical story of Ezekiel mentioned earlier. Minister Farrakhan relayed that he was picked up by a beam of light from a smaller ship and taken to a larger ship. There, he had a chance to meet with the Honorable Elijah Muhammad. He was instructed to inform Colonel Muammar Qadhafi of Libya that there was going to be a bombing of his capital and a personal attack and that other plans were being made to accelerate a Third World War. Minister Farrakhan did inform Colonel Qadhafi of the plans. It was reported that when the bombing took place, there was a tremendous amount of interference that caused some of their airplanes to malfunction. A group of small saucers reportedly had been hovering over the area.

Alien Profiles

Let's now examine a few types of extraterrestrials. The first category of such entities includes the ones who oversee the mother-ships: the demigods. One type comes from the North Star and beyond. If you could see them, you would immediately notice their fiery bodies. They are very tall, approximately eight feet in height. They have tremendous mystic powers. They are able to move at the speed of the mind and have the extraordinary ability to be able to see what we are doing at any time. There are many categories of demigods who reside in the higher planetary systems.

The second classification of alien beings is called the "gray" type. They are depicted as very short with large black eyes, big oval heads, thin bodies and vestigial mouths, noses and ears. This type carries out the majority of the abductions. One major book about abductions is *Communion* by Whitley Streiber. It details UFO contact in which people have been abducted and subjected to various types of experiments, resulting in a change of consciousness. Examinations are typical of UFO abductions. The examination involves exploring and probing the abductee's body with elaborate machines. Instruments are inserted in the body, particularly in the nose and rectum. Humans who have been abducted in this way later experience pain or consistent bleeding in the nose.

Some people who have been abducted have dreams of being raped or of being on a spaceship and ejaculating continuously. These dreams represent their real experiences. The abductors take semen and use it for the continuation of their own race. Humans who have had their seed taken during these experiences later feel pain in the genitals. If you have had recurring dreams of associating with something otherworldy and have experienced the problems just mentioned, then you may have already been affected by these beings. But don't fear; these entities are not necessarily negative. They are a sad case. They have minimized the ability to love and thus have evolved without loving tendencies. Having evolved into a state where they are basically composed only of intelligence, they have no emotions. This is why their heads are big and their bodies are small. They use their mental capabilities to abduct; they paralyze their subjects through mental telepathy. These entities have a very deep involvement and interaction with this planet. Part of their preoccupation with this planet is due to their desire to acquire emotions.

Another classification of aliens are those found at the center of the earth. Some of these aliens are not humanoid while others, such as those descendants of the "lost continents" of Mu and Atlantis [see chapter eight], are humanoid. During the fall of Mu and Atlantis, some residents were guided by the mother-ship to take shelter at the earth's center. Surprisingly, some unidentified flying objects do not necessarily come from other planets but from the core of our own.

There are also those extraterrestrials who are of a definite negative nature. They rebel against the divine order and negatively affect earthly arrangements. They are sometimes called demons. There are humans who maintain contact with these negative extraterrestrials. These personalities have consciously evolved into tyrants. They are trying to control the minds of people on this planet for personal power and the amassment of slaves. They encourage people to engage in scams, initiate wars and participate in satanic worship. These tyrants have highly placed agents in governments all over the world and have more control than the secret societies. They have infiltrated secret societies as a means to exercise their powers of control and manipulation.

This planet is controlled by secret societies such as the *Illuminati* and the *Skull and Bones* Society. *Skull and Bones* is one of the most powerful organizations in existence. Its members involve themselves in human sacrifice in order to gain power. Members of the *Illuminati* have immense knowledge about demigods and extraterrestrial beings. They contact negative entities through meditation and other types of metaphysical powers. As they call upon these entities, they are supplied with various metaphysical weaponry, for the purpose of control and domination. Through government agencies such as the Trilateral Commission, the Federal Reserve, and the International Monetary Fund, etc., these societies work their agenda of control and manipulation, in full view of the world's population.

Government Secrets

As mentioned, numerous reports exist about extraterrestrial experiences. Many people feel that the government has made strong attempts to conceal this information from the public. However, it is no longer possible to keep a lid on this topic. There have been many exposés of the 1947 incident in Roswell, New

Mexico, where townspeople reported viewing a disc-shaped flying object. Military personnel were called in and some observed the wreckage of this crashed object. Over a hundred people, mainly those associated with the government, were aware of the crash. This case was particularly interesting because people also reported viewing bodies of the extraterrestrials in the wreckage. The descriptions were of the gray type of beings mentioned earlier. The incident was officially reported as a crashed weather balloon. Years later, several former government officials appeared on television and stated they were instructed to keep the incident secret and were threatened with potential loss of employment if they did not comply. The officials eventually spoke out because they could no longer keep this information secret.

It is now accepted by a certain contingent of society that ex-president Eisenhower experienced extraterrestrial contact. It is reported that ex-president Carter also saw UFOs. One of the parliamentary members of the House of Lords in England, the Earl of Clancarty, who is also involved in the dissemination of information about extraterrestrials, spoke to a pilot involved in an extraterrestrial incident at Edwards Air Force base. The Earl has written on this subject in no uncertain terms.

We can see just from these few examples that extraterrestrial contacts and UFOs are a wide-spread phenomenon; they are not limited to a few "kooks." Groups of people who have had these experiences meet on a regular basis. They discuss the effects of the experiences on them and their families and the ways they are coping. There is also a UFO hotline in New

York that makes information available to the public about the recent sightings and experiences that have occurred. We must realize the urgency of the situation and be aware of what is happening in these areas. The next few decades may have a very devastating impact on us if we are not prepared.

Seeking a Life of Love

If I have merely stirred your interest in extraterrestrials or increased your fear, then I have failed in my purpose. The issue is this: to what degree is this information enhancing your ability to appreciate the controlling hand of the Lord behind everything that exists? Is it encouraging you to surrender to His control? If this information helps you to realize the desperate need to develop greater love, then this discussion has been successful. When higher beings decide whom they will salvage or help, they look at the degree of loving energy that a person has embodied. Anyone who is contacted by a mother-ship who has low vibratory energy or a low consciousness will not be able to adjust to the contact. However, those who are already living a life of moral purity and compassion have made large deposits into their "spiritual bank accounts," and are in a position to properly receive a mother-ship.

Once you are in harmony with God it becomes His duty to ensure your survival. It is His duty, too, to see to your protection. It becomes His agents' duty and joy to do His bidding in relationship to you. However, if you are not constantly calling out to Him, the alternative scenario is bondage. You become the victim of those negative forces that influence our minds via the mass media. By constantly bombarding you with stimuli designed to arouse your material desires, they successfully bring you down to a lower level of consciousness, where they can harass and control you.

This is one of the most incredible times to be a part of this universe. Entities are here who have been waiting millennia for the opportunity to be born at this time, just so they can gather enough spiritual momentum to carry them back home to the spiritual world. You also have purposely taken birth at this time on this planet to be a part of this unfoldment. We encourage you to align yourself with people and practices that will raise your consciousness and that will harmoniously align you with the universe and with God.

Question: I once met someone who had detailed knowledge about UFOs. He said that the first nuclear catastrophe was Sodom and Gomorrah. Could you elaborate on this?

Answer: Yes, the story of Sodom and Gomorrah is an example of what happens when nuclear energy is released. The mother-ship had a duty to perform and it performed it. All of these events are based on the aggregate free will and the collective consciousness of individuals. What happens to each person is based on individual *karma*. If you have the kind of protective karma that is generated by being a righteous person and by being in harmony with God, then even if your life is taken there is a science by which your soul can be brought back into your body if necessary.

Question: Is the Creator a force that determines the outcome of our consciousness or is it the choices we make, our own creativity, that lead us to be positive or negative?

Answer: It is definitely a matter of our creativity. The Supreme Lord is like a supreme parent who loves every aspect of His children and who is constantly making options available for them according to their receptivity. God does not have any favorites. A person's desires will dictate whether that individual is attracted to the pious polarity or the impious polarity. How we use our free will determines our choices and how we draw or repel various situations. As we sow, so shall we reap. Under the law known as the conservation of energy, the third law of motion in physics, every action produces an equal and corresponding reaction. We are completely responsible for the things that are happening in our lives. If we really understood this, we would be much more careful about the way we interact with each other, with the world around us, and with God.

Question: I have been studying UFOs for a considerable time, yet most of the information you are sharing with us today I have not read anywhere. I wonder whether I have been wasting my time because I have learned more in the short period of this lecture than in all my years of studying.

Answer: Some of the things that we are discussing you will not find in books. Much of this information was made available through contact with a level of cosmic attunement as well as a connection from a previous life. We are summarizing tremendous amounts of knowledge in an attempt to make it available for your growth. It would be difficult for you to discover this information by just reading various books. The nature of the knowledge we are sharing with you is not necessarily for the mind; it is meant to go deeper. Our words are being planted like seeds in the heart and consciousness. The soul knows the truth and it has the ability to identify and align itself with the desire of each person as each individual searches for the higher truths.

7
Strangers in Our Bodies

This body is a vehicle that can experience an infinite number of situations. The Vedic Puranas speak of 8,400,000 types of bodies that the soul can occupy throughout the creation. If we accept the fact that the soul is the real person, and that the body acts as a costume or garment, we can understand that we change costumes according to the activities that we have to perform from one moment to the next, from one life to the next. If the body can be changed, then death is nothing more than a visit to the changing room. We merely leave one set of clothes behind and put on another. The law of conservation in physics tells us that matter can neither be created nor destroyed, but that it simply changes form. So although our bodies are changing from childhood, to youth, to old age, something remains the same. That something is the spirit soul. This discussion will examine situations where one's body accommodates different types of temporary or permanent visitors.

Walk-Ins

We first will discuss walk-ins. A walk-in occurs when a person no longer wants to continue life in the present physical form. The individual departs and *willingly* allows another soul to occupy his or her body. A good analogy might be "time sharing:" one soul is occupying a form that can be used by another. The original owner of the body usually desires to leave because of depression, frustration, or anxiety.

One may also decide to leave the physical form temporarily and allow another entity to occupy it. This practice has gained popularity over the last decade under the name of channeling. Channelers are people with the ability to act as mediums. They receive communication from other realms, act upon the messages and encourage others to act. This should not be shocking. History shows that many great inventors and others who have made major contributions to society heard voices and were given certain instructions from other realms.

Beings who walk in come with their own unique patterns, but are simultaneously aware of the patterns of the previous occupant. The entities who enter in this way are generally of a positive or pious nature. They are still evolving, yet they have a duty to perform in bringing about a new era. Their understanding and their nature assist them in these efforts. The advantage of entering a body in this way is that it saves time. The walk-ins do not have to undergo the process of birth and growth; they can immediately begin the work they are to do. Sometimes they may not know that they have entered this life as a walk-in; at a later time this fact is revealed. One indication that such a transition has taken place is when someone who has had a period of distress or has given up the will to live abruptly changes patterns of thought and behavior.

Possession

Possession is the forceful occupation of one's body by another entity, typically a negative entity. As mentioned, walk-ins are invited voluntarily. Sometimes entities that enter under possession may also be invited by the host, but this invitation is reflective of the host's low level of consciousness. When individuals eager for wealth, distinction, and power are ready and willing to sell themselves for this power by associating with lower entities and lower vibrations, such lower beings can penetrate them. The intruding personality is dominant over the host entity. Unlike the walk-in phenomenon, the host entity still occupies the body with the visiting entity.

In the past few years, there has been an increasing number of people who have committed horrendous crimes such as mass murders and serial killings. Many of these people, when brought to justice, have reported hearing voices and receiving "instructions." This is not hallucinatory; their nature has allowed negative beings to reside within their consciousness. In fact, they often say that they did not want to do certain things but that they were feeling pushed to act in a particular way.

Disembodied entities often attempt to occupy the physical bodies of others. Because they are preoccupied with gratifying their senses, they try to engage in negative sexual activities and other forms of manipulation. These entities dabble on the astral plane and are often encountered during sleep. Those entities that engage in sexual activities are called *incubi* and *succubi*.

A symptom of an obvious attack would be when one feels something trying to enter the body through the chest or through the back of the neck. A subtle attack may be indicated by the occurrence of "wet dreams." The sensations of waking up and not being able to speak, or of being awake and asleep simultaneously, can indicte that a disembodied entity is trying to enter.

Entities will occupy the bodies of people who make themselves available through particularly sinful lives or fearful dispositions. However, without these preconditions, these entities can have no effect. Seventy-five percent of the work in becoming free of a possession is recognizing that it is there. Certain characteristics accompany states of possession. Some examples include heavy odors, lower room temperature, or the levitation of objects. Exorcism is one means of inducing the entity to leave.

Entities of a negative nature have power just like entities of a divine nature. Miracles, such as apparently supernatural acts, are not necessarily a sign of divinity. Contact with lower entities for the purpose of acquiring supernatural power is a phenomenon common in the Caribbean, South America, and Africa. In Benin, West Africa, a high percentage of the women reveal low-level possession. In most cases their families committed their offspring to water spirits before the children were born. Thus, many people from that area, especially women, become inhabited by such entities. They hear annoying voices and are often drawn to the water. We have assisted some in severing the attachments.

To minimize the possibility of possessions, one should not attend any rituals involving the shedding of blood, illicit sex or attempts to communicate with the dead. Much of what is practiced as African religion in the United States is an adulteration of the bona fide practices. At the current level of consciousness on the planet, ceremonies that deal with flesh and blood sacrifices are not going to invoke a divine presence or divine consciousness. Those who find themselves receptive to subtle energy should be wary of situations where these practices occur because such environments are permeated with negative energy. This energy can be imbibed on a very deep level, resulting in possession.

Critical Information for Critical Times

Because of their limited exposure and deep cynicism, Westerners tend to be ignorant about altered states and other dimensions. They are normally insensitive to or unaware of anything more than their immediate reality. Thinking that this immediate environment is the "be-all and end-all," they tend to ridicule alternative realities.

This perspective is not beneficial. People should be open to these types of realities. We are the generation that must determine the viability of the future for humankind. We are living at a time when the entire planet is in danger. This predicament demands more advanced solutions and tools to counteract the problems that are eating away at the next generation. Under such conditions, there is a thin line between those who will survive and those who will not.

We are risking credibility by making information of this type available, yet the gravity of the world situation demands that these things be made known. Many of you, as responsible leaders for the future, will need this kind of knowledge. As mentioned earlier, no one is living at this time by accident. It is part of our *karma* to be on this planet at this particular time. It is critical to train and cultivate leaders in the techniques that will be needed to instruct and direct the masses, not just to a higher standard of living, but ultimately to the path of higher spiritual realizations. Those who have learned to operate at a higher vibration and with a higher consciousness will bring about a new era that will soon be more evident. God's mercy is greater than His law. He is more eager to send messages and teachings then we are ready to receive. Since God is so eager to give, we are often given information beyond our capacity and qualification. That is His mercy; that is His love.

Question: If individuals work at enhancing their vibrations through the proper diet, would that not make them less vulnerable to intrusions by other beings?

Answer: Yes. Factors such as how we think, how we act, and how we relate interpersonally determine the kind of energies drawn to us. Diet is vital not only because it affects how the body functions but because it influences our thoughts and actions as well. Proper diet combined with chanting *mantras (powerful words)* and prayers greatly elevates the consciousness. It affects the vibrations of the body and allows us to develop greater fortitude.

Question: When you spoke about entities within us, it brought to mind the feminine and masculine that is within us all. Could you talk about the importance of developing the feminine and masculine qualities of God within ourselves so we can be in a better position to receive spiritual assistance?

Answer: The feminine, nurturing aspect of ourselves becomes more dominant as we become more spiritual. The world is experiencing the effects of an overexertion of the masculine aspect which minimizes the nurturing, the receptive, and the metaphysical. The perfectly balanced, wholistic stage of development involves an androgynous outlook where both the masculine and feminine aspects are exhibited. God contains everything and as we adopt a more Godly orientation, that universality is seen within us and within those beings that are here to help.

Question: Can the way we feel about ourselves and the world we live in make us more, or less, prone to possession by negative entities?

Answer: Yes, it can, because the more negative we are and the less we love ourselves and others, the lower our vibrations become. This causes us to attract negative things. By positive living and thinking, we can avoid attacks on all levels.

We have been conditioned to believe that gratifying or appeasing our senses is the goal of life. This sense gratification can be gross, such as illicit sexual activity, or subtle, such as the desire for profit, adoration and distinction. When we encounter obstacles that limit our sense gratification, we feel that our lives are over. The knowledge being shared here is to help you realize that there is a much more expansive perspective on life. The challenges that make your life more difficult, at the same time propel you towards greater growth.

Believe that if you have disappointing experiences, you can move beyond them. View bouts of negativity as if they were seasonal changes. Just as there is summer, fall, winter and spring, problems come and go at regular intervals. Any circumstance we are in is only temporary. Focus on the fact that you will have better days in the future. Material energy is relative. In a relative world, happiness is always followed by distress and vice versa. The wise person learns how to function in good times and bad. The wisest person learns how to change even a negative situation into a positive one. The more we operate in this fashion, the more we will attract pious beings and experiences into our lives.

8
The Pyramids: Ancient Structures of Mystery

There are not many subjects today that generate as much interest, speculation, and conjecture as the pyramids. For centuries, the best archeologists, pyramidologists, and Egyptologists have had difficulty explaining them. The approach that will be taken here is not a typical historical analysis or a sociological evaluation. Our goal is not to subtract from the significant amount of research that has been done in this area by competent scholars. Instead, we want to take you in another direction, one that examines the spiritual implications of the pyramids.

Interesting and Amazing Facts

The word "pyramid" itself stimulates great interest. It has been written that a rice-cake of a particular shape was popular in ancient Greece. Referred to as *pyramis*, some believe it was the origin of the word "pyramid." The most logical root of the word comes from the interpretation of the Greek words *pyro*, meaning fire, and *mesos*, meaning middle, referring to the fire rituals that the ancient Greeks observed in the stone structures they visited in Kemet (Egypt).

The *Encyclopedia Britannica* states that the Egyptian name for the pyramid was *mer* or *meru*. An interesting fact is that the name *meru* is also found in the ancient Kushite and Vedic cultures. The word Kushite is the term used to describe the inhabitants of the land of Kush. The original dark-skinned people occupied the area that is now part of northeastern Africa. In the Kushite culture, there is the ancient capital known as Meroe, and in the Puranas, the mountain of the gods was called Meru. This dwelling place of the demigods is described in the Bhagavata Purana as a pyramid-shaped peak. This leads to the view that the pyramid shape is representative of Mount Meru.

Pyramids exist not only on the African continent but also in Central and South America, Mexico, Kampuchea, Ethiopia, Somalia and India. The presence of these structures around the world highlights the fact that at one time a single world culture existed consisting of a single empire known as the Kushite empire.

More than eighty pyramids were built along the banks of the Nile in ancient Kemet. The size of the pyramids is astounding. The Great Pyramid of Giza built for King Khufu contains more than two and a quarter million stone blocks, each block weighing an average of two and one-half tons. It originally stood 481 feet and covered a base of thirteen acres. The

Pyramid of the Sun in Teatihuacan, Mexico had even a larger base than the biggest pyramid in Kemet.

The structure of the pyramids includes many chambers. There are tunnels, like a subway, that connect the Giza pyramids underground. Some of these tunnels lead into the innermost part of planet earth. It has been documented that a river of water can be found in the base of the pyramids. This water is of spiritual significance, since it represents the barrier between the material and the spiritual worlds.

The pyramids are so awe-inspiring that they have long been placed among the seven wonders of the ancient world. The pyramids amaze both scientists and laypersons. Much information can be gained about the cosmos through the study of the construction and function of the pyramids. Many experts believe that the pyramids are so significant that, once they are understood, much of the mystery of human existence on this planet will be explained.

Who Were the Egyptians?

It is often wondered whether the pyramids were built by people like ourselves. Even with the best technology, we cannot produce even a small replica of the Great Pyramid. The Nikon company of Japan once tried without success to build a sizable pyramid using modern technology. One mishap after another forced them to abandon the attempt. The more we understand who the Egyptians were and with whom they were connected, we can understand how it was possible for them to create such magnificent structures and why they cannot be duplicated now.

The scriptures tell us that in ancient times there was a single land mass that covered the earth. In the Bhagavata Purana, it was called *Jambudvipa*. It is often referred to as Gondwanaland. This land mass was divided into nine sections, called continents or *varsas*, by different mountain ranges that were part of the central mountain, Mount Meru. The bulk of Meru is now buried within the body of the earth with only the peak visible. Of the nine continents, only seven remain visible; the other two were submerged during the last continental shift and realignment of the earth. The two "lost" continents were popularly known as Mu and Atlantis. It is believed by some that the Egyptians were descendants of the people of Mu. Others propound that they were products of the earlier Kushites who existed in Nubia, Ethiopia, and the Sudan.

The people of Mu and Atlantis had great metaphysical abilities. They were God-conscious, highly sensitive, loving, communal, and very spiritually attuned. The Atlanteans were experts in mysticism and energy conversion and were intellectually and mentally advanced. They were not, however, as spiritual as the people of Mu.

The land of Mu was destroyed by a change in the earth's axis. After Mu fell, some of the people migrated to Atlantis. Atlantis was also later destroyed. Both downfalls were accelerated by misuse of mystical knowledge. After these two land masses were destroyed, most souls left their bodies and went to other planets or universes. Some souls were forewarned and took shelter in the inner earth; these entities became the ones to "reseed" the planet. This is similar to situations now where some leaders have been warned to relocate their communities in certain areas to prepare for oncoming calamities. As a new phase of human civilization began again on earth, those who remained on the planet propagated the species. Some souls who had left their bodies during the destruction returned. Those souls who took shelter in the inner earth did not immediately become part of the activities on the surface. The offspring of those who propagated the species naturally inherited higher knowledge about the cosmos. A significant segment of the people of Egypt possessed this ancient knowledge. This explains a paradox that often challenges historians: there was never a time when the ancient Egyptians were primitive; they were always at a high level of achievement.

People of the Inner Earth

Every planet is populated inside as well as outside. God is so fantastic that life can be found everywhere. The entities from the inner earth are very close to us. They have gained much wisdom because they fled from the activities of war and natural catastrophes. They were able to survive because their consciousness is one of compassion and love. Because they are of a subtler nature, they are not always manifest in this plane. They can choose whether they want to be visible or not.

Beings of the inner earth have the ability to visit here. Using energy conversion, these beings have the ability to create force fields that can penetrate the ocean, opening it up to allow their vessels to come in or out. An example is the Bermuda Triangle. The ships and planes that disappear involve the inner earth people. Sometimes inner earth personalities cause volcano eruptions and hurricanes as a reaction to the testing of nuclear bombs in the their atmosphere. At other times, there is a need for them to release a particular energy that often manifests in the form of earthquakes or volcanoes. The real reason for this phenomenal activity, however, is the collective *karma* of the individuals on the planet itself.

The ancient Egyptians were related to the beings of Mu and Atlantis and had full knowledge of the beings of the inner earth. They were very powerful beings with great knowledge and extraterrestrial contacts. Much of what was accomplished regarding the pyramids was due to these connections.

The Building of the Pyramids

There are numerous and varied accounts of how the pyramids were built. The Greek historian Herodotus asserted that groups of 100,000 men worked for twenty years to build the Great Pyramid. Other perspectives are that 4,000 skilled laborers worked all year round. Many have the conception that the stones were dragged up ramps that grew as the pyramids rose, and that the ramps were later dismantled. Some researchers question these theories. For example, some say that in order for the ramp theory to be true, the ramps would have to be more sophisticated than the pyramids themselves. They would have to be expanded and extended so fast that it would be impossible to build the pyramids.

Information regarding how the pyramids were built is known by some secret societies, especially the Masonic order. The major architect of the pyramids was Imhotep. He was responsible for much of the knowledge of the mystical schools. Imhotep was considered to be an incarnation of the son of God and thus was in the same category as Jesus—an empowered representative of the Godhead. For about two and one-half years, Imhotep planned the construction of the major pyramids. The actual work took less than six years. How is this possible when scientists, basing their estimates on present-day technology, claim that the Great Pyramid could not have been completed in less than twenty years?

One key aspect was the use of laser energy for cutting the stone. This explains the smooth cut of the blocks that amazes scientists. Another critical aspect was that through the process of converting energy and raising vibrations, the Egyptians were able to counteract gravity and literally levitate the stones with minimum expenditure of human energy. This is how the construction of the pyramids was possible. To many people, this perspective may seem highly unlikely, but consider the vast amount of knowledge our contemporary scientists have acquired with much less capabilities and connections than the ancient Egyptians. Realistically, then, there must have been knowledge of superior technologies that is untapped by present-day minds.

The Pyramids: Places of Worship or Tombs of Death?

There has been widespread speculation about the purpose of the pyramids. Much has been made about the presence of the bodies of the pharaohs found in the inner chambers of the pyramids and the great wealth that was placed with them. This has led to the perception that the pyramids functioned as elaborate burial chambers for the dead. However, the purpose of the pyramids was much greater than this.

The main function of the pyramids was to worship the Supreme and the many demigods that served Him. The ancient Egyptians considered themselves descendants of the sun, part of the dynasty of the sun. Ancient cultures considered themselves descendants of either the sun or the moon. This is the case with the people of Somalia, for example, where *soma* means moon, and *Ali* means God. Kilamanjaro is known also as the mountain of the moon. In Egypt, worship of the sun was prominent, *ra* being the name for the sun. In sanskrit, *ra* means "shining light" or "brilliant." The Bhagavata Puranas state that people generally worshiped the Supreme Lord in the form of *Surya Narayana*, who is the sun god.

Pyramids were used as temples in which fire sacrifices and rituals were performed. The pyramid was like a miniature universe in that it represented the structure of the universe, from the subterranean planets through the heavenly planets and upwards into the spiritual realm. The spiritual world was represented by the zenith, or tip, of the pyramid in which was encased a black stone, or amanite, a representation of the Supreme Lord. It is interesting to note that in the Egyptian language, the words *amen* or *amonon* mean "concealed," and similarly in sanskrit, the same word *amonon* means "God-hidden." Both *aum* and *amonon* in the Vedic culture represent Divinity or God in a hidden form.

Another of the major functions of the pyramids was to act as a navigating element for extraterrestrial beings. When they were first built, the pyramids were coated with limestone and could be seen for miles and miles. The pyramids were like amplifiers allowing communication between the priests and these beings. The perfectly executed construction allowed such communication to take place. This communication between those on earth and other beings was not unusual at that time. The elaborate and precise worship in which the priests of the temples engaged created an atmosphere conducive to contact with the demigods. Not only did the demigods come and go freely, but they had personal exchanges with earthly beings. These relationships were possible because of the purity of consciousness of the earth inhabitants. As the collective consciousness became less God-conscious and more degraded, these types of exchanges diminished in frequency.

Transition of the Soul

To better understand why bodies were placed in the pyramids, one must examine Egyptian philosophy. The Egyptians believed that because the pharaoh was a representative of God, he would become a god at his death. Therefore, they were very particular about the arrangements made for him both in life and death. Once the representative of God left the body, he was placed in a shrine called a *samadhi* or "place of final trance" in his own assigned chamber within the pyramid temple structure. This was done because the king or pharaoh was considered a divine representative of the Supreme Godhead. Because his body was considered to be spiritualized, it could not be disposed of in an ordinary manner. This practice of placing the representatives of God in special burial chambers still occurs in modern-day India for spiritual masters, since they are considered revered saints. These *samadhis* are found in the temple structures and become places of pilgrimage for those seeking spiritual advancement.

The Egyptians believed in the concept of the *ba* and the *ka*. The *ba* is the soul and the *ka* is a spiritual duplicate of the physical body. The *ka* is spiritual in nature, created at birth and released by the body at death. The Egyptians believed that the soul, the *ba*, remained within the mummy of the pharaoh in the heart region and that the *ka* would travel between the material universe and the spiritual universe. The *ka* could come back and forth as long as the physical body could be recognized, so often a statue of the person would be placed in the tomb and a mask in the likeness of the person would be placed over the mummy.

The Egyptians believed that once a person was entombed, the journey to the chambers of judgment would begin. At the end of that journey, the soul's past activities would be judged by a karmic board, which would determine one's next life based on the activities during one's past life. One's consciousness and commitment to service would be factors considered by the board. The god Anubis would weigh the heart of the deceased person against the feather of Ma'at, the goddess of justice. The more negative *karma* a person had accumulated, the heavier was the heart. If the heart was too heavy, it would outweigh the feather and the heart would be consumed by a monster. In this conception, the soul then would become an evil spirit forever in opposition to the gods. If the heart passed the test, then it would go to live with Osiris in *Yalu*, the heavenly kingdom.

There is an evident connection between the Egyptian culture and that of Sudan, Ethiopia, and Ghana. For example, there are many similarities between the inner activities of the pharaoh and that of the Asante Hene (the cultural president of Ghana). This is not surprising, because history tells us that when the Egyptians left Egypt, they migrated to Sudan and Ghana, where some of the knowledge of the ancient practices is still available. We have personally observed these similar practices in our exchanges with the Asante Hene. There is always a person seated at the right foot of the Asante Hene, representing his soul. This person is usually a young boy called the *kra* which means "soul" in the Akan language. In Egypt, when the pharaohs left their bodies, they usually did not go alone; some close attendants were sent with them. When the Asante Hene leaves his body, those personal attendants closest in service to him will leave with him. Until recently, a hundred others also had to leave. When the Asante Hene leaves his body, his departure is usually not announced for awhile. When it is announced, those individuals who are to leave with him have already been chosen. Those persons who are part of the internal entourage have been trained for this role; they are to be attendants in the hereafter. Thus, practices that existed thousands of years ago are still operating now.

Deity Worship: An Idol Occupation?

The temples of ancient Egypt held magnificent statues that the Egyptians worshiped. They had the understanding that a living essence dwelt within those statues. The Bible condemns idol worship, but this practice was not idol worship. Idol worship exists when people create something from their own imaginations and then worship that concoction as God. In one sense, idol worship is anything that you consider more important than God, whether it's your car, your house, or your job—anything that takes priority over serving the Lord.

Confusion has developed concerning the difference between idol worship and deity worship. Many people mistake deities for idols. In deity worship, *mantras* are recited that invite a spiritual presence into what, by external appearance, would seem to be wood, stone, or marble. Just as the wind can come into a building, certain spiritual elements can come inside a physical structure. The soul is inside the physical body, yet when the soul leaves, the body is called a corpse. The confusion occurs when the uninitiated think that the external form is the spiritual essence itself.

The Priests' Daily Practice in Deity Worship

Many religious traditions have some kind of form that they worship. Reverence for the icon serves as a catalyst for spiritual growth. Originally, deity worship had authorized standards describing how the priest was to construct the statue and authorized techniques for worshiping it. If you were to travel back in time and witness the daily worship of the deity in Egypt, you would observe very precise, purposeful devotional activities. Before sunrise the god's meal would be prepared, and at dawn the priests and priestesses would awaken the god with melody and song as they went in procession to the shrine. The priests that had undergone purification entered the shrine and proceeded to bathe, dress, and decorate the deity with costly ornaments. They then burned sweet incense and offered the food and drink they had prepared. The food, now considered sanctified, was removed and later distributed among the priests. At midday and in the evening, further meals were cooked and offered to the deity, and at night the deity was put to bed. The room was purified by incense and was carefully swept and put in order for the next day's activities.

By studying the daily lives of the temple priests, we can understand that they were not involved in a whimsical activity concocted from their minds. Their lives reflected the authorized techniques and rituals with which they worshiped the deities. The priests were allowed many privileges, but they were also expected to lead simple and austere lives. They had high standards of cleanliness and were to eat and drink moderately, abstaining from certain foods such as pork and fish. They bathed twice a day and shaved their heads and bodies every three days. Their clothes were simple fine white linen cloth and they wore white sandals.

Not all priests were allowed to perform deity worship. They were authorized by spiritual masters. There were several levels in the priesthood assigned to each demigod; some priests wore distinctive clothing to show their position. The priest who was responsible for the chanting of the *mantras* always wore a sash across his chest. These daily practices of an ancient priesthood can be seen today in the lives of the brahmin priests of South India and the fetish priests of West Africa. Even today many of these practices remain intact. However, due to the low consciousness in present-day human civilization, it is recommended that people not involve themselves in deity worship to the same degree as in the past.

Mystical Mantras

There are two principal *mantra* techniques, both of which involve repetition. One is verbal repetition, and the other is a written form. Both are very potent in affecting the consciousness. This art of *mantra* repetition is known to people of the different mystery schools who have acquired this confidential knowledge. They write certain *mantras* on their own bodies or chant certain *mantras* to ward off negative energy and attract positive energy.

In Egypt, when death rituals were performed, the priest would write various *mantras* on the chest of the mummy. The priests would also write *mantras* for protection on amulets and place them around the neck of the mummy. The Egyptian Book of the Dead, also known as The Book of Coming Forth By Day, explains certain rituals on how to "open the mouth." This does not refer to the physical mouth, but to the calling of the *ka* into the statue of its owner, endowing the statue with the faculties of a living person. This was all done by the power of *mantras*, or *hekau*, written on the body of the mummy or on the person's statue. When you chant a *mantra*, you are invoking the energy with which the *mantra* is associated. This is similar to when you call someone's name; you are bringing that person to you.

Mantras also provided protection in the tombs so that when intruders entered the tombs, they fell prey to a curse. In many cases, grave robbers died when they broke into the tombs. The deaths of the intruders were arranged by two mechanisms. The first involved the priest making a potent force field by chanting *mantras*. Second, the priests were so astute in science that they could arrange for radiation to affect the cells of a person passing through it, causing an immediate reaction.

Mantra chanting is so potent that certain ancient priests could take someone's life through incantations. Even today, there are people, especially in India, Africa, and South America, who know the science of chanting *mantras* and can heal the sick through the process of sound vibration. Before ceremonies for certain rites of passage were performed, the priest would recite specific *mantras* so the participants could recognize the priest's power.

We should always remember that activities such as *mantra* chanting and deity worship should be under taken in the mood of "Lord, Thy will be done." These spiritual technologies actually allow us to make spiritual connections to help our consciousness focus on the will of the Lord, understanding that the Lord is actually always here for us.

Revealing the Function of Secret Orders

Some mystery schools had to practice underground to protect the ancient wisdom, making it
available to initiates only. They knew the dangers
associated with offering this knowledge openly: common people would abuse its power. Historically,
these secret orders would not expose certain truths,
but instead kept them in an inner circle. This practice is not elitist. Members knew that people could
harm themselves and others if confidential knowledge fell into the hands of the uninitiated. An example is animal sacrifice, which was a legitimate ritual
carried out by qualified people under certain conditions. By taking the life of the animal, the priest
could either send the animal to a higher realm or
arrange for that animal to receive another body of a
higher order. Thus, it was an activity of liberation.
Now people are performing animal sacrifices without the proper knowledge or consciousness, thereby
bringing about unwanted negative effects on themselves and the environment.

The priests in the pyramids of Egypt had tremendous knowledge and power, but the knowledge
became fragmented as the planet went through
upheavals and the priesthood became polluted
through corruption and political manipulations. The
knowledge eventually became diluted and degener-
ated into many of the religious institutions seen
today, with their ecumenical councils and mundane
interests. The leaders gradually began to change one
aspect after another until the original tradition was
no longer recognizable.

Ancient Structures: Modern Teachers

The pyramids and the activities therein were like shrines for broadcasting spiritual messages and making spiritual contact. They allowed for amplification of thoughts and communication with higher entities for the invocation of certain blessings and, later, for preparation of the body for its connection with the worlds after physical death.

The pyramids assist us in appreciating the deep knowledge that is revealed as we go within ourselves and penetrate deeper levels of consciousness. The pyramids also keep us aware of the communication and cooperation that can exist among the different planes of activity. These magnificent structures remind us to connect back with our Source, the Supreme Lord, in order to be empowered to do the work necessary for spiritual upliftment of the planet.

Question: Please explain the effects of *mantras*.

Answer: Sound has effects on matter. You can manipulate matter to such a degree that it begins to change form. A soprano can sing a note that, held long enough, can shatter a glass. The sound vibrations of different qualities have different effects on consciousness and different effects on matter. These effects can be seen even with music. Certain types of music make one aggressive, lusty or excited. Other types of music enhance relaxation and sleepiness. Thus, sound affects the consciousness just as it affects matter. It affects the subtle body; it has an influence on how the molecules and cells function. There are specific sounds that have specific effects; these sounds can be channeled and used to raise consciousness or to lower it.

Question: Given the information shared about ancient Egypt, how can those who identify with Egypt best direct their studies of Egypt and their travel to Egypt for optimum spiritual growth?

Answer: If you project your consciousness on Egypt, then you project your consciousness on the universe because the people of Egypt had major control of the whole planet. They came from different time periods and they had knowledge of the entire earth. They even had connections with other planets. This knowledge reflects the conception of "act locally but think globally" because they directed their energies towards their immediate activities, yet also had an expansive vision and arena of activity.

You should also act locally and globally and think in interplanetary terms. Because you have to be practical, you act locally but don't allow yourself to be stagnated. In that way you are including more variables of reality and considering how they interrelate and interact. You then will be more aligned with the laws of the Supreme and will be more able to follow those laws.

Question: It seems that pyramids are becoming a fad in that many people are focusing on "pyramid power:" putting objects under pyramids or sitting under pyramids seeking mystical experiences. I've experienced those types of things but the thrill has worn off.

Shouldn't we be looking for something higher than exciting experiences?

Answer: This is a very good point. Sometimes when we are new on the spiritual path, the Lord gives us unusual experiences. Certain psychic phenomena occur, or we experience a little bliss. Then, after awhile, everything disappears and we begin chasing after that experience, trying to recapture it. The Lord gives us a little taste of what is possible in order to heighten our desire and to encourage us to keep moving forward. However, the goal should not be mere metaphysical or psychic experiences; they can become distractions. Although they are often needed to demonstrate the existence of something beyond our usual experience or to encourage us to explore more subtle levels, at a certain point they are no longer important. Metaphysical and paranormal phenomena will occur around us without our trying to pursue them. Pursuing them can lead to dependency and may become addictive, just as if we were taking a drug. In such circumstances, the desire for power and control, and for unusual abilities, ultimately pushes love for the Supreme to the background.

As we grow spiritually, we begin to learn that real progress happens internally. Various guides, such as books, teachings, and physical or spiritual personalities, are available to help us measure our progress. All of these help us look at ourselves from different angles to discover the right course of action, which ultimately is to move aside and allow the Lord to lead. This process does not require us to give up our identity, to be slaves, or to be meek and submissive. Instead, it asks us to develop a faith strong enough to allow us to say one day, "From this day on, dear Lord, I am yours," and to truly mean it. Then everything becomes available to us. Eventually, we reach the point of realizing that we have been trying to be in the driver's seat for so many lifetimes. For so many lifetimes we have been seeking what we want and not what we need. Sometimes we have even received what we wanted, only to discover that we were still not satisfied. The object of our desires was not what we expected, and sometimes it even complicated our situation. After such a process continues for a very long time, finally one day we say, "Dear Lord, Thy will be done. I give up trying to understand reality in an independent way, and I no longer think I can perceive and control everything with this limited mind." It is this mood of "Thy will be done, Lord" that allowed the priests in ancient Egypt to utilize rituals in ways that were spiritually potent. The more we can imbibe this surrendered consciousness, the more we can advance on our spiritual paths towards the goal of increased love and service to the Lord.

9
The Quest for Eternal Bliss

*A*key emphasis in scriptures from various paths is developing our relationship with God. Unfortunately, people often have limited information about the object of their love—God's likes and dislikes, His activities, His abode—and how to connect with the Lord. Comprehensive information about these topics is available and we will share some of it in this discussion. Follow carefully; certain things will be exposed that will later emerge in your consciousness at those times when it is most needed.

Four Universal Paths

How do we connect with the supreme goal? What path will take us back home? To begin with, all paths fall into four philosophical categories: *materialism*, *voidism*, *impersonalism*, and *personalism*. It is important to keep these four schools of thought in mind as we examine what is in the material universe, what is outside the material universe, and what is in the spiritual kingdom.

The philosophy of materialism is basically an atheistic philosophy. Materialism holds that a human being is nothing but a physical entity without a soul. Existence is simply a matter of being placed in different environments which produce a corresponding personality. Life is viewed as simply a matter of eating, sleeping, mating and defending, or as Charles Darwin stated, a survival of the fittest. This philosophy produces gross selfishness and is based on exploitation and manipulation, rather than living in harmony with nature. This is the atheistic philosophy that the forces of oppression adhere to and try to spread throughout the world.

Secondly, there is the philosophy of voidism. According to this philosophy, material involvement produces anxiety, material relationships bring pain, and material pursuits cause stresses, frustration, and depression. This connects deeply with the philosophy of Buddhism, where the goal is one of trying to obtain *nirvana*: freedom from ego, freedom from a focus on the material world, and freedom from the bombardment of sensual interferences. This philosophy tells us what reality is not, but there is little information on what reality is.

The third philosophy is that of impersonalism. Impersonalism moves us outside of the material arena and into cosmic consciousness or *samadhi*. In this consciousness, people experience the universality of all creation and feel a certain oneness with God, thinking themselves to be God. The focus is on merging into God's energy and on becoming one with the light of God. The philosophy of impersonalism tries to encompass all the basic material elements, but it explains only one dimension of Divinity, and is thus incomplete. It shows how we are one with God, but it totally neglects to explain how we are different from God, and this is essential. It is this difference that we experience and which stands out as fundamental for spiritual development. If we are different from God, then we can develop an attitude of service to Him. Otherwise, loving service becomes quite impossible.

The philosophy of personalism recognizes that materialism brings pain and confusion, but that one must rise above these difficulties and become free from sensual bombardment. The philosophy of personalism includes aspects of materialism, of voidism, and of impersonalism. But it goes further. It recognizes that there are some activities that are not material.

Let's consider an analogy. A man has a cavity which is causing a toothache. He is not even able to appreciate the aroma of food without his tooth hurting. Materialism is like an aching tooth; it gives a great deal of pain and suffering. The man tries mentally to rise above the pain and he also takes medication, which stops the pain for awhile. This level is like voidism: although he is free of the pain caused by the tooth, his state is one of neutrality at best. As the man focuses on enjoying the aroma of the food, he is at a level akin to impersonalism; he can enjoy the energy of the food. Once the man makes up his mind and goes to the dentist and is cured of the toothache, not only can he smell the food; he can actually enjoy eating it. This level is analogous to personalism. The elimination of the root cause of his suffering allows him to have a direct relationship with the food. Sometimes when we find ourselves in a bad situation, we think that "positive" means the elimination of the negative. However, to stop our negative material situation is merely the beginning. The next stage is to find some positive spiritual engagement to replace the material activity.

Personalism Versus Impersonalism

Personal conceptions automatically contain and go beyond impersonal understanding. The Supreme Lord, being absolute, can simultaneously exist personally and impersonally. There are three basic energies of the Divine: the external energy that maintains the material universe; the marginal energy, which is made up of the living entities; and the internal energy, which maintains the spiritual world. Due to our conditioning, we tend to view spiritual as the opposite of material. To us, material means form; therefore, spiritual must mean formless. Material means active; therefore, spiritual means devoid of activity. In order to grasp a true understanding of activities in the spiritual world, we have to lay these misconceptions aside. Through love and devotion, we can move beyond the impersonal approach to God after many, many lifetimes of being in this cosmic consciousness. We then finally obtain an opportunity to come in contact with the extraordinary activities of the spiritual world.

The spiritual world is our natural environment. The great teachers are constantly telling us about an existence beyond that which we perceive. They are anxious to show us the means to regain that most precious state that we have lost. For so many lifetimes the soul has been wandering in and out of many environments and situations, unconsciously starving for spiritual association.

When we say the prayer "Our Father, Who art in heaven, hallowed be Thy name. Thy kingdom come, Thy will be done, on earth as it is in heaven," we understand that the material world is a reflection of the spiritual world. The material world is actually a perverted reflection of reality. In the material world, we have many kinds of interactions, but they are limited, painful and, ultimately, lead to frustration. In the spiritual kingdom, our relationship is with the Lord and our activities are ever fresh. Every second in the spiritual world becomes a moment of higher pleasure.

There are two major divisions in the spiritual kingdom. There is the brahmajyoti, which is sometimes referred to as the light or effulgence, and there are the spiritual planets, where the various manifestations of the Lord and His devotees reside. God's personal aspect is experienced here. Some of you are still seeking oneness, the impersonal light, and the opportunity to merge with the Supreme. This desire is due to some material contamination. It is the first phase that we experience as we begin to make connection with the higher consciousness. As we experience cosmic oneness, we may become so intoxicated and happy that we falsely conclude there is nothing higher. This is our first major mistake. While these experiences are enjoyable, they are limited. Beyond cosmic consciousness is the opportunity for personal exchange with the Lord.

"Liberation" is a term frequently used in impersonal schools of thought—liberation from the material world to become one with God, or even to *become* God. Again, our goal should be beyond liberation. We must be liberated countless times before we get a chance to actually enter the kingdom of God. We must travel through many lifetimes and pay tremendous dues—pursuing austerities, religiosity and spirituality of various types—to get beyond the platform of liberation.

There is an intermediate phase of unfoldment when we are able to associate with an individual form of God located in the heart region of every living being; this aspect of God is known as the *paramatma*. This is a higher "oneness" that is more localized and more personal, a stage that great *yogis* strive to attain through their yogic practices. We can then spiritually advance towards the ultimate association with the Supreme Lord in the spiritual world.

Going back to the toothache analogy, once the aroma of food permeates someone's nose, the desire to eat the food will sooner or later become the uppermost goal. That person will then try all means possible to attain the food and enjoy it. Similarly, impersonalism will eventually lead to personalism. The question is: will we take the long, slow route of sense enjoyment or the direct, quick route of surrender to the Lord's will? The latter gives eternal pleasure.

Five Types of Relationships with God

As mentioned, the spiritual world is full of activities centered on loving exchanges with the Lord. Existence means functioning and interacting. The ultimate expression of all such functioning and interaction is love. Love involves service. Love does not simply mean knowledge about someone, nor does it just culminate in salvation. Once again, love means service. All the activities in the spiritual world are based on service to the Lord. Ancient scriptures tell us that there are exchanges we can have with God other than He as our father and we as His children. The Vedas detail the activities in the kingdom of God and speak of five relationships, or *rasas*, that we may have with the Supreme.

We can use the analogy of an invalid lying in bed. The relationship between the bed that the invalid is lying on and the invalid himself would be considered the first *rasa* of neutrality. In this *rasa*, which is one of serving in a non-active mood, the bed is serving the invalid neutrally. A servant brings in the person's meal. This servant is serving in the second *rasa* of servitude, where there is a certain amount of exchange, but on a very formal level. Then the person's friend walks in to visit; this is the third *rasa* in the mood of friendship and involves more warmth and personal exchange. Then the person's mother walks in to check on the situation, representing the *rasa* of parenthood which carries with it a whole different, more intimate set of emotions. Finally, the person's spouse returns home and serves the person in the conjugal *rasa*, or the intimate mood of a lover. As we move from the mood of neutrality to conjugality, the intimacy expressed between the giver and the recipient increases, as does the confidential nature of the exchange.

Another analogy is that of a judge. Most people view a judge with awe, reverence and fear. The colleague of the judge, who is also a judge, sees the judge as a friend. The two of them share a certain love and respect for each other in an exchange of friendship. When the judge goes home, he puts aside his role of judge for that of husband and father. He helps his wife wash the dishes and plays "horsey" on the floor with his grandchildren in a very loving mood. The intimacy of love pushes the relationship beyond the boundaries of formality. It goes beyond selfishness and produces an intensity in giving and sharing of a most personal nature.

The spiritual kingdom is a realm of intimacy, of deep sharing, and selflessness. Just as we experience relationships here, once back in the spiritual realm our relationships will be similar, but will be focused on God. In the material world we are all moved constantly by lust, which is literally forcing our actions and covering much of our activities with greed. In the spiritual kingdom, because we are in contact with the Supreme Personality, all of our actions are still being driven, but they are being inspired by love. There is a tremendous unconditional love so powerful that we are immersed in it, fully realizing ourselves as pure spirit souls.

The relationship of strong love among a mother, father and child that we see on earth is possible only because it exists in the spiritual world, in the realm of perfection. The material relationship is a reflection of the spiritual. In the spiritual world, we can act as the parent or friend of God. We can also have a conjugal relationship with the Lord in the mood of husband and wife. These relationships are all possible. Each of us has our own specific relationship. Once we are back home, it will be fully manifest. This type of personal interaction produces an amazing and almost inconceivable sense of ecstasy that increases as we render service to the Supreme Lord and His associates. The more we serve God, the more He serves us, encouraging us to serve more. Thus, the blissful reciprocation goes on. This information is very, very confidential. To those uncommitted to a spiritual way of life, descriptions of this highest state are kept to a minimum. As one's desire to know absolute truth increases, more knowledge is revealed.

Service is the highest ecstasy. Service can extend to a point where one finds feelings of ecstasy interfering with one's service. This symptom occurs in the highest of loving relationships. The experience of bliss in the spiritual world is so intense that talking is like singing and walking is like dancing. Every object in the kingdom is alive and possesses personality. There are trees that fulfill any desire you may have. Your desires, of course, are centered on God's pleasure; your desires are not only yours but His also. And this gives you even more pleasure. In the spiritual kingdom, there is no death, no disease, no old age; these occurrences are all part of this temporary world of limitations and pain.

We can go up to the heavenly kingdoms many, many times and enjoy them for thousands of years, yet we will ultimately fall back down. We can progress to the point of liberation hundreds and hundreds of times, but until we develop freedom from envy and until we obtain help from the ambassadors of the spiritual kingdom, there is no possibility of further progress. It cannot be achieved on one's own merit. However, one may have sufficient merit and a strong enough desire to attract one of the necessary helpers who will guide one to the actual kingdom of God.

Contact with an agent of the Lord from the transcendental realm is a rather unusual experience, since most souls simply entangle themselves further in the actions and reactions of materialistic life. It takes a tremendous amount of previously acquired pious credits from past lives to be given the opportunity to break the cycle. What actually happens when one is able to meet with a transcendental agent, or spiritual master? At that most fortunate time, one is given the opportunity to understand how to break out of this material existence and to experience the activities of the spiritual world. We should eagerly listen to and follow the instructions from such empowered agents of the Lord.

The Joy of Personal Exchange

Our desires bring to us what is necessary for our growth. Everything we experience is based on our desires, and our desires are based on the kinds of association that we keep and the type of vibrations that we imbibe. If we surround ourselves with people and activities of higher vibrations, the truth will naturally have its effect. That effect will vary according to the degree of envy we are holding within our hearts. We can have personal exchanges with God, even in these bodies. When this happens, the physical body cannot properly contain the experiences. There is a whole science of the ecstasy that one experiences when love of God actually awakens. For example, there are moments when one loses external consciousness. There are moments when the body begins to feel such happiness and love in contact with the Reservoir of Love that the limbs begin to retract like a turtle's.

A person who is beginning to have such experiences, and is beginning to have an awareness of past, present and future and of other dimensions, does not reveal such symptoms but keeps them confidential. The experiences are like a permanent "high" of tremendous intensity, but one that is difficult to share. Even the experience of coming in contact with the universal energy pales in comparison to having association with the spiritual world itself. The experience of the oneness of cosmic consciousness is like pain compared to the experience of transcendental activities in the spiritual realm. It could be said to be like searching for broken glass in a diamond mine.

Now these experiences may sound very unusual. That is because they *are* unusual. They are coming from other realms. Although they may sound very strange, there is a certain truth that many recognize. A certain part of our being has known intuitively of these truths, and now hearing them strikes a chord. Those of you who have encountered the concept of merging with God and have not been comfortable with it's ultimate goal of loss of identity, now know why. This concept *is* unnatural. We all have identities, fashioned in God's image, and we are consciously or unconsciously striving to reach the perfection of that identity.

In very advanced spiritual experiences of various traditions, we find references to the "bride of God" or to personal exchanges with the Lord. There were very advanced Muslims and Sufis who went beyond the rituals and experienced the great divinity of personhood. There were those in early times involved in mystic Christianity who spoke about hearing God. They were not imagining this. Because they were free of all obstacles, they were able to be natural. It is natural to be able to have communication with the Father. This entire discussion is just to help us gain greater realization that there are deeper levels for which we can strive. Certain seeds have been planted to help you gradually revitalize your dormant consciousness.

Question: You refer to scriptures from around the world, yet we know that scriptures have been corrupted throughout history by humankind. How does one go about analyzing what is true in the scriptures and what is not true?

Answer: We know that as history progresses, there is a tendency for humans to abuse and misuse scripture. We see this occurrence in scriptures that have many versions reflecting different interpretations, such as the Bible. While the basic essence remains, there are changes. All scripture can be appreciated and understood at different levels. There is always a need for a key to help us go deeper into a particular scripture. Three checkpoints help us understand truth in a particular scripture, although none of these by itself is sufficient and reliable. The checkpoints are: 1) the authorized scripture itself, 2) previous and current followers who are living the traditions of that scriptures (saints), and 3) the spiritual master, or *guru*. Any highly spiritual process has to balance all of these three elements. A scripture that is not in accordance with the teachings of the saints and masters is a bogus or watered-down scripture. Any saint whose behavior does not match the scripture and does not correspond with the teachings of the spiritual masters is a bogus saint, or at least some of the activities in which that person engages are bogus. Any spiritual master whose behavior does not correspond with the saints and bona fide scripture is a bogus spiritual mentor. When actions correspond with scripture, with saints living the tradition and with beings—spiritual masters— who have transcendental contact, we can feel secure. Whenever any of those checkpoints is out of line, we are at best adhering to something that, while functional, may not necessarily be of an absolute nature.

There are some teachers who say there is no need for books. They say this simply because they don't want to be checked. There are some "saints" who say there is no need to adhere to previous traditions or claim that there is no need for spiritual mentors. This is because they want only their ideas to be accepted. They, too, are bogus. There are some people who only follow scripture, and their minds are boggled by the apparent contradictions. They may read a scripture over and over and become confused or misinterpret its meaning. That is why, in addition to the scripture, we have living saints who are following the tradition, and ascended masters or prophets. We put these together and when they match, we know we have a bona fide prophet, a bona fide saint, and a bona fide scripture. Thus, although scriptures differ from each other and have been changed, the essence is still there and can be extracted.

Question: I have been searching for my true personality, my true inner identity that comes from God. What advice can you give me about how to find a guide to help me realize who I truly am?

Answer: It's very simple. Sometimes we get a little caught up trying to decide who is the right teacher or the best teacher. We don't need to reflect so externally. Instead, we should focus more on trying to become more serious in our own lives. As we are becoming more serious in our own lives, the Supreme Lord will connect us with the kind of teacher that can help us to the next stage. Don't worry so much about externals. Be serious within your own consciousness. Cry out more in desperation and that will naturally and automatically draw a master who will be able to guide you and help you at your present level. There are many different types of teachers, varying in quality and level of responsibility, simply because there are many different types of personalities who need to be helped in various ways. That is just how personally the Supreme Lord arranges everything.

Question: The uplifting of consciousness you mention seems to become more of a reality as the earth cleanses the impious elements. How long will it take before the cleansing is over and what will the earth look like once it is completed?

Answer: It's almost over now. Souls currently on the planet literally have come to be a part of this intense scheme of activity. Many have come from different types of universes and different types of environments to be here at this time to assist in what is about to take place. A description of the future cannot be so easily categorized because the future is taking place now, through the changing consciousness. I realize that this all sounds rather cryptic. However, we can say that we will not have the same kind of confusion and separatism of nationalism, racism, and tribalism to the degree that we do now. We won't have to experience the same limitations, because many of the limitations we are experiencing now are due to considerably low levels of consciousness. As consciousness becomes more elevated, we will have more opportunities to experience the higher realms. This will give us more ability to solve many of the problems that we now face. We will be more in harmony again with our "big brothers and sisters," the angels and demigods who have the responsibility to assist us. Resource depletion and shortages, which are all due to negative *karma* and sinful activities, will surely be a thing of the past.

As we develop a higher consciousness, the whole level of this planet will be raised. The bottom line is that people are getting a chance to see how much they are qualified for empowerment. With that empowerment, many of our dormant faculties will again become active. We currently use very few of our actual abilities and this is the reason why our consciousness is so dull. We have all types of psychic abilities that will enable us to function better in the coming world order. We can achieve a point where mental telepathy becomes commonplace. It is just a matter of being more in harmony with natural laws so that we are able to use more of what we have. These are incredible times for which we are preparing ourselves.

Closing Reflections

*C*reatures from the inner depths of this planet, splitting the earth with quakes and volcanoes; demons whispering in our minds feeding evil thoughts to our subconscious. Aliens from other universes and dimensions manipulating our lives; pyschic intrusion as an everyday reality; and subliminal suggestion as a staple of our existence. It seems like a bleak and sorry stay we have ordered for ourseleves on this earth planet. The situations just mentioned may seem far-fetched and outside everyday reality, but how bizarre are they? Any more bizarre than a mother crushing the skull of her five-year-old? Another strapping her toddlers into a sinking car? Fifteen-year-old youths slitting the throat of their peer in an outlandish sect-like ritual? Leaders being murdered for seeking peace? Civilians slaughtering each other en masse in the name of ethnic cleansing? This unfortunately is the reality, as extraordinary as it sounds. "What is to be done?" There are a number of options. We can succumb to the negativity and either jump on the band wagon or dive to the depths of depression, which usually ends in suicide or an addiction of some kind. We can take a neutral stance and opt out of the human race. We can become one of the mindless masses controlled by fear, intimidation, and manipulation.

There is another path: the path of the Spiritual Warrior. It is not an easy path. It demands courage, determination, discipline, intense compassion — and unconditional love. It requires an understanding that this world is not the final chapter. Spiritual Warriors undergo adversity and challenge, but in a positive and equipoised frame of mind, realizing that challenges purify and obstacles force them to jump higher, run faster, and try harder. Even gold, the most valuable and costly of metals, is brought into its glory by fire, and the diamond, the most precious of gems, is formed by intense pressure and heat. Spiritual Warriors are not alone; they carry the Supreme Lord in their hearts. Angels guard and guide them and the residents of the spiritual world cheer them as heroes and heroines on their journey back home to the transcendental realm. Do you want to join the ranks of this transcendental army? If so, you must take a stand; you must make a choice. As the negative forces struggle to maintain their foothold in our lives, only two sides will emerge: the spiritually enlightened and the materially oppressed. Beloved, you do not have the luxury of time. Your current thoughts and actions are already placing you in one camp or the other.

The earth will emerge into a millenium of spiritual enlightenment and purity. Her residents will be conspicuous by their loving natures and peaceful minds. The *devas* and angels will again visit this planet, and tranquility will permeate the atmosphere. We invite you to take your place among the inhabitants of the Golden Age. Take up your weapons of austerity, mercy, compassion and love, and join the ranks of the Spiritual Warriors as we forge a new beginning under the banner of the Supreme Lord.

Suggested Reading

This suggested reading list may further enrich your understanding of the subjects covered in this book.

Ali, Abdullah Yusuf. *The Meaning Of The Holy Qur'an.* Brentwood: Amana Corporation, 1993.

Amen, Ra Un Nefer. *Metu Neter (Vol. 1): The Great Oracle Of Tehuti and The Egyptian System of Spiritual Cultivation.* New York: Khamit Corp., 1990.

Budge, E. A. Wallis. *The Egyptian Book Of The Dead: The Papyrus Of Ani, Egyptian Text Transliteration and Translation.* New York: Dover Publications, 1967.

Carter, J. Edwin. *Living Is Forever.* Norfolk: Hampton Roads, 1990.

Downing, Barry H. *The Bible And Flying Saucers.* New York: J.B.Lippincott, 1968.

Grinder, John, and Richard Bandler. *Trance-formations: Neuro-Linguistic Programming and the Structure of Hypnosis.* Moab,Utah: Real People Press, 1981.

Spiritual Emergency: When Personal Transformation Becomes a Crisis. Edited by Stanislav Grof and Christina Grof. Los Angeles: Jeremy P. Tarcher, 1989.

Hadees-E-Qudsi (The Commands Of Allah). Edited by Sahbanul Hind and Hazrat Maulana Ahmad Saeed. New Delhi, India: Dini Book Depot, 1988.

Key, Wilson Bryan. *The Clam Plate Orgy And Other Subliminal Techniques For Manipulating Your Behaviour.* New York: New American Library, 1981.

————. *Subliminal Seduction: Ad Media's Manipulation Of A Not So Innocent America.* New York: Signet Books, 1981.

Kusche, Larry. *The Bermuda Triangle Mystery: Solved.* Buffalo: Prometheus Books, 1976.

Levi. *The Aquarian Gospel Of Jesus The Christ.* Marina Del Ray: Devors and Co., 1988.

Lewis, Byron A., and R. Frank Pucelik. *Magic Demystified.* Lake Oswego, Ore: Metamorphous Press, 1982.

The New Oxford Annotated Bible with the Apocrypha (New Revised Standard Version). Edited by Bruce M. Metzger and Roland E. Murphy. New York: Oxford University Press, 1991.

Montgomery, Ruth. *Here And Hereafter.* New York: Coward and McCann, 1968.

_____. *A Search For The Truth.* New York: Morrow, 1967.

_____. Strangers Among Us: Enlightened Beings From A World To Come. New York: Coward, McCann and Geoghegan, 1979.

_____. *Threshold To Tomorrow.* New York: Putnam, 1982.

_____. *The World Before.* New York: Coward, McCann and Geoghegan, 1976.

_____. *A World Beyond: A Startling Message From The Eminent Arthur Ford From Beyond The Grave.* New York: Coward, McCann and Geoghegan, 1971.

Muhammad, Elijah. *Message To The Blackman In America.* Chicago: Muhammad Mosque of Islam No.2, 1965.

Prabhupada, A .C. Bhaktivedanta Swami. *Bhagavad Gita As It Is.* Los Angeles: Bhaktivedanta Book Trust, 1983.

_____. *Easy Journey To Other Planets.* Los Angeles: Bhaktivedanta Book Trust, 1982.

———. *The Journey Of Self Discovery.* Los Angeles: Bhaktivedanta Book Trust, 1990.

———. *The Laws Of Nature: An Infallible Justice.* Los Angeles: Bhaktivedanta Book Trust, 1991.

———. *A Second Chance: The Story Of A Near-Death Experience.* Los Angeles: Bhaktivedanta Book Trust, 1991.

———. *Srimad Bhagavatam, Cantos 1-12* (Also referred to as the *Bhagavata Purana*). Manila, Phillippines: Bhaktivedanta Book Trust, 1982.

Rosen, Steven. *Food for the Spirit: Vegetarianism and the World Religions.* New York: Bala Books, 1990.

Strieber, Whitley. *Communion: A True Story.* New York: Avon, 1987.

———. *Transformation: The Breakthrough.* New York: Beech Tree Books/Morrow, 1988.

Subramaniam, Kamala. *Mahabharata.* Bombay, India: Bharatiya Vidya Bharan, 1990.

Thompson, Richard L. *Alien Identities: Ancient Insights into Modern UFO Phenomena.* San Diego: Govardan Hill Publishing, 1993.

Three Initiates. *The Kybalion: A Study Of The Hermetic Philosophy Of Ancient Egypt and Greece.* Chicago: The Yogi Publication Society, 1940.

Time-Life Books. *Mysteries Of The Unknown: Mystic Places.* Alexandria: Time-Life Books, 1987.

———. *Mysteries Of The Unknown: The UFO Phenomenon.* Alexandria: Time-Life Books, 1987.

African Presence In Early Asia. Edited by Ivan van Sertima and Runoko Rashidi. New Brunswick: Transaction Publishers, 1988.

Glossary

Acharya: A sanskrit word meaning one whose behavior reflects God, or one who teaches by his example. Another name for a *guru*, or spiritual master.

Astral traveling: Traveling in the astral or subtle dimension, or traveling with the astral body. A dimension accessible to us in our sleep state.

Aura: A field of fine sheaths of energy which permeate the solid physical bodies of molecules and atoms, producing a luminous glow surrounding a figure or object. This is often depicted as a halo around the heads of spiritually advanced beings.

Bhagavata Purana: Also known as the Srimad Bhagavatam. Ancient vedic scriptures of principal narrations and instructions dating back at least three thousand years. There are eighteen of them in number, of which the Bhagavata Purana is the most important.

Brahma: The first created being of the universe. Under the direction of the Supreme Lord, he creates the universe and all forms of life in the universe. He rules the mode of passion.

Demigod: More highly consciously evolved beings that act as agents of the Supreme Lord and are responsible for the day to day functions within this material universe.

Deva: Sanskrit word meaning demigod.

Hadees-E-Qudsi: Known also as the El Hadith, or Ahadith, consists of visions or words sent by Allah and revealed through the angel Gabriel which were described by the Prophet Mohammed in his own words. Scriptures which complement the Holy Koran.

Incubi: Female humanoid entities that engage in erotic relationships with human beings.

Kemet: The original name ancient Egyptians gave their land.

Mahabharata: The history of the planet. One of the vedic scriptures, along with the Ramayana known as the itihasas, (historical epics).

Mantra: Transcendental sound that frees the mind from material bondage.

Modes: Refers to the three qualities of material nature: goodness, passion and ignorance.

Muzak: Trade name for piped-in recorded background music available in public places.

Siddhi: A sanskrit word meaning mystical ability or perfection. There are eight principle siddhis that can be obtained through austere yogic training. These include that ability to make an object lighter than air, enabling it to float; the ability to reduce one's body size; the ability to expand one's body into nine duplicate forms; the ability to aquire an object from any where outside one's immediate enviroment immediately.

Sidratil Muntaha: The place where Allah resides.

Sucubi: Male humanoid entities that engage in erotic relationships with human beings.

Swami: A person in the fourth order, or *ashrama* of renunciation. One who is able to fully control his senses. Also refered to as Goswami.

Vedas: A sanskrit word meaning knowledge. The name given to the oldest collection of written manuscripts known to man.

Vimanas: Sanskrit word denoting aerial vehicles, which could be either grossly physical machines, made of subtle energy or transcendental (spiritual) energy.

Yuga: A sanskrit word meaning millineum or age. A portion of time designated to the spiritual seasons that occur on a cyclical basis in this universe.

Index

About the Author

S wami Krishnapada was born John E. Favors in a Christian, God-fearing family. As a child evangelist he appeared regularly on television. As a young man he was a leader in Dr. Martin Luther King's civil rights movement. He became president of the student council group at Princeton University and was also chairman of the Third World Coalition. His main degree is in psychology; however, he has many accolades covering such fields as politics, African studies, and indology. He is also a scholar of International Law.

His Grace has held several governmental posts such as Assistant Coordinator for penal reform programs in the State of New Jersey, Office of the Public Defender. He has been the director of several drug abuse clinics in the U.S.A. and has served as a campaign manager for politicians.

Swami Krishnapada has been a special consultant for Educational Testing Services in the U.S.A.

and gained international recognition as a representative of the Bhaktivedanta Book Trust, particularly for his outstanding work with the scholars of the then-communist countries.

He directly oversees projects in Washington, D.C., Detroit, and Pennsylvania (U.S.A.), West Africa, as well as South Africa. He is the director for the American Federation of Vaisnava Colleges and Schools, and His Grace is presently the only African-American Vaisnava Guru in the world.

In the United States, Swami Krishnapada is the founder-director of the Institute of Applied Spiritual Technology, director of the International Committee for Urban Spiritual Development, and one of the international co-ordinators of the 7th Pan African Congress. He is also a member of the Institute for Noetic Science, the Center for Defense Information, the United Nations Association for America, the National Peace Institute Foundation, the Global Forum of Spiritual and Parliamentary Leaders on Human Survival and the World Future Society.

A specialist for international relations and conflict resolution, Swami Krishnapada constantly travels around the world and has become a spiritual consultant to many high ranking members of the United Nations, various celebrities, and several chiefs, kings and high court justices. In 1990 His Grace was coronated as a high chief in Warri, Nigeria in recognition of his outstanding work in Africa and the world, and in 1994 and 1995, Swami Krishnapada met with President Mandela in South

Africa where they shared their visions and strategies for world peace.

Along with encouraging the process of self-sufficiency through the development of schools, clinics, farm projects and cottage industries, His Grace finds time to conduct seminars on stress & time management, and other pertinent topics. He is also acknowledged as a valuable participant in the resolution of global conflict.

ORDER FORM

Title	Price	QTY	Total
Spiritual Warrior: *Uncovering Spiritual Truths in Psychic Phenomena*	$12.95 + $3.00 s/h		
Leadership for an Age of Higher Consciousness: *Administration from a Metaphysical Perspective*	$23.00 + $5.00 s/h		
The Beggar: *Meditations and Prayers on the Supreme Lord*	$12.95 + $3.00 s/h		
Yearly Subscription to **Spiritual Warrior**: The *Quarterly Newsletter of the Institute for Applied Spiritual Technology*	$10.00		
		Subtotal:	
	MD Residents add 5% sales tax:		
(Please make checks payable to Hari-Nama Press) **TOTAL:**			

☐ **Please send me a free catalog of books, audio and video tapes.**
☐ **Please add me to your mailing list.**

Name:
Address:
City, State, Zip:
Telephone *(Optional)*:

HARI-NAMA PRESS
P.O. Box 4133
Largo, MD 20775
Telephone/Facsimile:
(301) 390-0672